→INTRODUCING

CULTURAL STUDIES

ZIAUDDIN SARDAR & BORIN VAN LOON

Published in the UK in 2010
by Icon Books Ltd.,
Omnibus Business Centre,
39-41 North Road, London N7 9DP
email: info@iconbooks.co.uk
www.introducingbooks.com

Sold in the UK, Europe, South Africa
and Asia by Faber and Faber Ltd.,
Bloomsbury House,
74-77 Great Russell Street,
London WC1B 3DA
or their agents

Distributed in the UK, Europe, South
Africa and Asia by TBS Ltd.,
TBS Distribution Centre,
Colchester Road, Frating Green,
Colchester CO7 7DW

This edition published in Australia
in 2010 by Allen & Unwin Pty. Ltd.,
PO Box 8500, 83 Alexander Street,
Crows Nest, NSW 2065

Previously published in the UK and
Australia in 1997 as *Cultural Studies for
Beginners*, and in 1999 and 2004 under
the current title

This edition published in the USA
in 2010 by Totem Books
Inquiries to: Icon Books Ltd.,
Omnibus Business Centre,
39-41 North Road,
London N7 9DP, UK

Distributed to the trade in the USA by
Consortium Book Sales & Distribution
The Keg House
34 Thirteenth Avenue NE, Suite 101
Minneapolis, Minnesota 55413-1007

Distributed in Canada by
Penguin Books Canada,
90 Eglinton Avenue East, Suite 700,
Toronto, Ontario M4P 2Y3

ISBN: 978-184831-181-7

What Is Cultural Studies?

Cultural studies is an exciting and "hot" field of study. It has become the rage amongst progressives of all sorts – not least because culture as a theme or topic of study has replaced society as the general subject of inquiry among progressives.

Cultural studies has made its presence felt in academic work within the arts, the humanities, the social sciences and even science and technology. It appears to be everywhere and everyone seems to be talking about it.

But what exactly is cultural studies? The term "studies" suggests a broad field of inquiry – like business studies or management studies. So is cultural studies simply the study of culture?

We know what business is. And what management is.

But culture? Well, that's an altogether different thing.

What is Culture?

The ambiguity of the concept of culture is notorious. Some anthropologists consider culture to be social behaviour. For others, it is not behaviour at all, but an abstraction from behaviour. To some, stone axes and pottery, dance and music, fashion and style constitute culture; while no material object can be culture to others.

Yet for still others, culture exists only in the mind.

One of the oldest definitions of culture was given by the British anthropologist, **Sir E.B. Tylor** (1832-1917) in the opening lines of his book, *Primitive Cultures* (1871):

Culture is that complex whole which includes knowledge, belief, art, morals, law, customs, and other capabilities and habits acquired by man as a member of society.

Here are a few more attempts to define culture ...

American anthropologist **Margaret Mead** (1901-78)

Culture is the learned behaviour of a society or a subgroup.

Margaret Mead

Raymond Williams (1921-88), one of the founders of cultural studies

Culture includes the organization of production, the structure of the family, the structure of institutions which express or govern social relationships, the characteristic forms through which members of the society communicate.

Clifford Geertz (b. 1926), Professor of Social Science at Princeton University

Culture is simply the ensemble of stories we tell ourselves about ourselves.

On the basis of these definitions, culture seems to be (almost) everything and cultural studies the study of (almost) everything!

What is the Subject of Cultural Studies?

Not surprisingly, cultural studies does not have a clearly defined subject area. Its starting point is a very broad and all-inclusive notion of culture that is used to describe and study a whole range of practices.

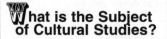

This makes cultural studies radically different from such conventional disciplines as physics or sociology or philosophy, each of which has its own clearly demarcated subject area or object of study.

Apart from the ambiguous nature of its subject area, cultural studies also lacks its own principles, theories or methods.

But it does have its own very distinct and distinctive history.

If cultural studies does not have its own theories or methodology, how does it actually function?

Cultural studies functions by borrowing freely from social science disciplines and all branches of humanities and the arts. It appropriates theories and methodologies from

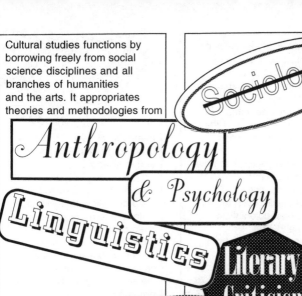

Sociology

Anthropology

& Psychology

Linguistics

Literary Criticism

AND ART THEORY

Musicology

Philosophy

and Political Science.

Almost any method from textual analysis, ethnography and psychoanalysis to survey research can be used to do cultural studies.

Cultural studies takes whatever it needs from any discipline and adopts it to suit its own purposes.

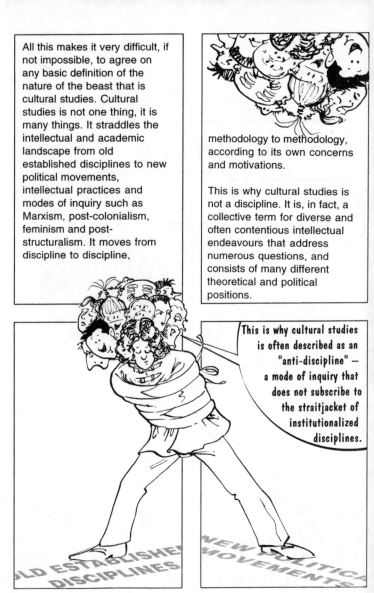

All this makes it very difficult, if not impossible, to agree on any basic definition of the nature of the beast that is cultural studies. Cultural studies is not one thing, it is many things. It straddles the intellectual and academic landscape from old established disciplines to new political movements, intellectual practices and modes of inquiry such as Marxism, post-colonialism, feminism and post-structuralism. It moves from discipline to discipline, methodology to methodology, according to its own concerns and motivations.

This is why cultural studies is not a discipline. It is, in fact, a collective term for diverse and often contentious intellectual endeavours that address numerous questions, and consists of many different theoretical and political positions.

This is why cultural studies is often described as an "anti-discipline" — a mode of inquiry that does not subscribe to the straitjacket of institutionalized disciplines.

OLD ESTABLISHED DISCIPLINES

NEW POLITICAL MOVEMENTS

Characteristics of Cultural Studies

Just because cultural studies is practically impossible to define, it does not mean that anything can be cultural studies or cultural studies can be just anything. The history of cultural studies has provided it with certain distinguishable characteristics that can often be identified in terms of what cultural studies aims to do.

1. Cultural studies aims to examine its subject matter in terms of *cultural practices* and their *relation to power*. Its constant goal is to expose power relationships and examine how these relationships influence and shape cultural practices.

2. Cultural studies is not simply the study of culture as though it was a discrete entity divorced from its social or political context. Its objective is to understand culture in all its complex forms and to analyse the *social and political context* within which it manifests itself.

3. Culture in cultural studies always performs two functions: it is both the *object* of study and the *location* of political criticism and action. Cultural studies aims to be both an intellectual and a pragmatic enterprise.

4. Cultural studies attempts to *expose and reconcile the division of knowledge*, to overcome the split between tacit (that is, intuitive knowledge based on local cultures) and objective (so-called universal) forms of knowledge. It assumes a common identity and common interest between the knower and the known, between the observer and what is being observed.

5. Cultural studies is committed to a *moral evaluation* of modern society and to a *radical line* of political action. The tradition of cultural studies is not one of value-free scholarship but one committed to social reconstruction by critical political involvement. Thus cultural studies aims to *understand and change* the structures of dominance everywhere, but in industrial capitalist societies in particular.

How to do Cultural Studies: Semiotics

To understand how cultural studies is done, we need to equip ourselves with a few of its key concepts and principles.

A major concept in cultural studies is that of **sign**. A sign has three basic characteristics.

It has a concrete form.

It refers to something other than itself.

And it can be recognized by most people as a sign.

The physical form of the sign is known as the **signifier**...

...what the sign refers to, its mental association, is known as the **signified**.

This linguistic theory of the sign had its impact in the 1950s and 60s as the intellectual revolution known as **Structuralism** which affected anthropology, psychoanalysis, literary criticism, Marxism and much else, and remains vital to subsequent **post-structuralism**.

The theory of signs developed from the work of Swiss linguist, **Ferdinand de Saussure** (1857-1913). He argued that language is a cultural phenomenon; and it generates meaning in a special way. Language produces meaning by a system of relationships, by producing a network of similarities and differences.

The principles which govern linguistic systems also organize other types of communication systems, such as writing, film and fashion.

The way we dress, what we eat and how we socialize also communicate things about ourselves, and thus can be studied as signs.

Saussure's followers developed a study of signs – **semiotics** – to establish the basic features of signs and explain the way they work in social life.

Signs, Codes and Texts

Signs are often organized as **codes** governed by explicit and implicit rules agreed upon by members of a culture or social group. A system of signs may thus carry **encoded** meanings and messages that can be read by those who understand the codes. A signifying structure composed of signs and codes is a **text** that can be read for its signs and encoded meanings.

Text can only be fully appreciated if seen in _context_.

When the social and power relationships are examined, the historical forces shaping the text are understood.

The combination of signs and significations is considered, and the general environment within which the text exists is recognized.

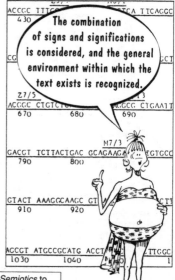

Readers are advised to consult _Introducing Semiotics_ to orientate themselves in this crucial subject.

Representation of the Other

The process, and the products, that gives signs their particular meaning is **representation**. Through representation, abstract and ideological ideas are given concrete form. Thus the idea/sign "Indian" is given a specific ideological shape in the way "Indians" have been represented in colonial literature – in the novels of **Rudyard Kipling** (1865-1936) and **E.M. Forster** (1879-1970) for example – as cowards, effeminate, untrustworthy.

The representative entity outside the self – that is, outside one's own gender, social group, class, culture or civilization – is the **Other**.

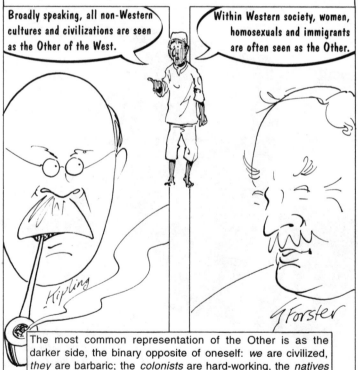

> Broadly speaking, all non-Western cultures and civilizations are seen as the Other of the West.

> Within Western society, women, homosexuals and immigrants are often seen as the Other.

The most common representation of the Other is as the darker side, the binary opposite of oneself: *we* are civilized, *they* are barbaric; the *colonists* are hard-working, the *natives* are lazy; *heterosexuals* are good and moral, *homosexuals* are immoral and evil.

Discursive Analysis

The notion of **discourse** binds all these concepts into a neat package. A discourse consists of culturally or socially produced groups of ideas containing texts (which contain signs and codes) and representations (which describe power in relation to Others). As a way of thinking, a discourse often represents a structure of knowledge and power. A **discursive analysis** exposes these structures and locates the discourse within wider historical, cultural and social relations.

Let us apply these concepts to a concrete example — the restaurant in the photograph.

What signs and codes does it contain? What culturally significant meaning is it communicating?

Decoding the Indian Restaurant

We can see that "Raj Balti" is located in an ordinary London street. The words "Take Away" tell us something of its status: a working-class restaurant in a working-class area. "Raj" in the name suggests a colonial link to India (it could also be the name of the owner!). The word "Balti" too has significance. But what, exactly?

To explore what our text is telling us, let us put "Raj Balti" in context – in relation to other Indian restaurants, their history and cultural significance in Britain. The Indian restaurant made its presence felt in Britain in the 1950s after the arrival of immigrants from the Subcontinent.

Now the word "curry" itself has a history. It was a sought-after commodity in the Middle Ages. When the Mughal Emperor Jahangir granted permission to Sir Thomas Roe in 1605 to establish a company in India, it was specifically for exporting Indian curries and spices.

Four hundred years later, after colonization had done its work, and the Indian Others had been represented in a specific way, curry came to signify the lowest form of cheap food, equivalent to chips, which it has replaced as the most popular food item in Britain.

The Indian restaurant itself was seen and represented as a monolithic entity. *All* restaurants serving food from the vast continent of India were "Indian restaurants". But "eating Indian" incorporates eating a diverse variety of distinctively different foods from India, Pakistan, Bangladesh and Sri Lanka; Punjabi, Mughal and South Indian dishes; "veg or non-veg". But to the British, everything was "curry". Until the 1970s, "going for a curry" had a special meaning. It was what the lads did when the pubs closed and they were looking for somewhere to vomit their intoxication.

But Indian restaurants have also resisted. In the first instance, the resistance simply exploited the ignorance of the white patrons. Curry you want, curry you get: the same curry was served with different labels. So someone eating *rogan gosht*, chicken *masala* or prawn curry was eating exactly the same thing with different bits of meat!

The word "Balti" gives us a clue to the second form of resistance.

> Balti is a receptacle, a pitcher, a pail for carrying water for washing or taking a bath.

> In the Subcontinent, it is often used to flush the old-fashioned squatting lavatory.

It is clearly too deep, too wide, too rough and too undisciplined for the preparation of a varied and sophisticated cuisine like the "Indian". So what is the relationship between Indian restaurants and balti?

Balti plays a significant role in how the Indian restaurants have sold "authenticity". When white patrons became more knowledgeable and realized that "curry" was a generic term describing a vast variety of foods, authentic Indian food became associated with a *tandoor* – the oven in which it was supposedly cooked.

In the 1970s, all good and authentic Indian food was prepared in a tandoor.

Tandoor gave way to <u>karahi</u>, the wok, which was all the rage in the 1980s.

The 1990s became the age of the <u>balti</u>.

The "balti" in "Raj Balti" signifies the restaurant's "authenticity" and trendiness.

Actually, a karahi pretending to be a balti

More generally, balti hides a subtle transformation that the restaurants from the Subcontinent have experienced and are experiencing. The selling of balti, as a renovated traditional and authentic "Indian", is a way for the Subcontinental restaurants both to reposition themselves in relation to British society and to reclaim their history.

By attaching different labels to basically the same food, the Indian restaurant broke out of its working-class image and acquired a fashionable label. The great leap of the balti is not unlike **Marcel Duchamp**'s (1887-1968) helping leap for the humble urinal.

Now you find my urinal among the artistic masterpieces of Europe.

And we have éliticized Indian cuisine so that the balti can now sit among the cordon bleu pots of the Western civilization.

The names of the restaurants are codes that reveal the changing power relationship between Indian restaurants and British society. In the 1960s, Indian restaurants had names like "Maharajah" and "Last Days of the Raj". These names were designed to rekindle fond memories of the empire that had recently been lost.

During the next phase, the names changed to "Taj Mahal" and "The Red Fort". These invoked images of the rich history and tradition of the Indian civilization, masking British pretensions to possession of an empire while reclaiming their own history.

In the third stage, the names shed their colonial connections. They reveal not only the infusion of new ethnicities but also a certain self-confidence that invites Indians to eat Indian: "Lahore Karahi" and "Bombay Brasserie".

In the most recent phase, the Subcontinental restaurants have again changed their names to indicate authenticity of expression and a confidence of having arrived: "Jalabi Junction", "Café Laziz" and "Soho Spice".

In many of these restaurants, the cooking area is part of the dining experience, providing assurance not just of freshly-cooked food but also bringing back the direct and tactile relationship between the hand that cooks and the hand that eats.

Moving from discursive analysis to interpretation, we can conclude: in arriving at its latest culturally legitimate state, the "Indian" restaurant has performed a genuinely authentic miracle. It has cosmopolitanized and humanized a very parochial and sanitized people.

There is more than one way to colonize a population!

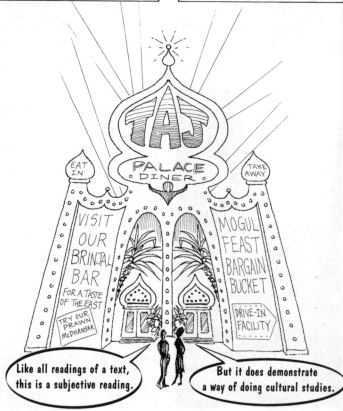

Using such methods, cultural studies has analysed all varieties of cultures:

High Culture
Low Culture
Public Culture
Popular Culture!
Mass Culture
Rock Culture
Youth Culture
Black Culture
Black British Culture
GAY CULTURE
Style Culture
Cyber Culture
Colonial Culture
Post-Colonial Culture
Postmodern Culture
GLOBAL CULTURE ...

Indian Kulcha?

And all varieties of cultural forms and practices:

ART
ARCHITECTURE
ADVERTISING
LITERATURE
MUSIC
FILM
TELEVISION
THEATRE
DANCE...

23

Origins of Cultural Studies

The name "cultural studies" derives from the **Centre for Contemporary Cultural Studies** (CCCS) at the University of Birmingham, established in 1964. In 1972,

the Centre published the first issue of *Working Papers in Cultural Studies* with the specific aim "to define and occupy a space" and "to put cultural studies on the intellectual map". Since then, the work done at the Centre has acquired a mythological status in the field.

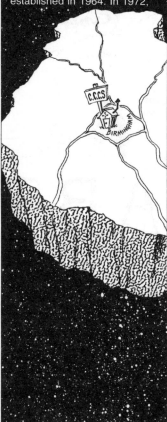

The works of **Richard Hoggart** (b. 1918), **Raymond Williams** (1921-88), **E.P. Thompson** (1924-93) and **Stuart Hall** (b. 1932), all of whom were associated with CCCS at various times, are regarded as the foundational texts of cultural studies.

Founding Fathers
The writings of the founding fathers arose from a particular social and historical context.

We all came from working-class backgrounds and taught at adult education institutes.

We were concerned, in our different ways, with the question of culture in the class-based society of England.

Each of us tried to understand the role and effect of culture at a critical point in England's own history.

The Second World War had just ended, educational opportunities within Britain were being extended and adult education was being promoted as a means of post-war reconstruction. But pre-war class politics was still the norm in a changed and rapidly changing social environment. Moreover, Britain was being invaded by popular American culture that shaped public consciousness and highlighted the class-ridden character of English cultural life.

Working-class intellectuals like Hoggart and Williams saw their task as endorsing the culture of common people against the canonical élitism ("high culture") of the middle and upper classes. They celebrated the "authentic" popular culture of the new industrial working class.

'Ere's another one, missus...

But working-class enthusiasm for American mass culture is problematic.

We're concerned not with how people accommodate to passively inherited culture ...

But with what people *do* with the cultural commodities they encounter in their daily life.

Their focus was on how culture is *practised* and how culture is *made* – or how cultural practice leads different groups and classes to struggle for *cultural domination*.

Richard Hoggart

Richard Hoggart started his academic career as an adult education tutor at the University of Hull. As professor of English literature at Birmingham University, he founded the Centre for Contemporary Cultural Studies. His book *The Uses of Literacy* (1957) gave cultural studies its first identifiable, intellectual shape. Basing his work on **F.R. Leavis**'s (1895-1978) ideas on literary criticism, Hoggart argued that a critical reading of art could reveal "the felt quality of life" of a society. Only art could recreate life in all its rich complexity and diversity.

And only art can allow us to move outside the time-dependent fabric of daily experiences.

But the working classes are caught between artistic and media élites.

The dominant élite expressed their power by giving legitimacy and exposure to *their* cultural forms and practices – by projecting their "fields of value". Cultural struggle thus involved a war for legitimacy and cultural status.

Authentic Working-Class Life

Hoggart describes the "authentic" working-class life and culture of pre-war Britain as an interconnected whole —

the pubs and the working-mens' clubs merged neatly with family structure, language patterns and community activities, creating a rich, organically connected life.

He contrasts this nostalgic view of urban working-class life, often described in personal terms, with the mass culture...

...of imported American pop music and television programmes, comics and crime and romance novels.

♪ SINCE MAH BAYBAH LEFF-MAH ♪

The mass culture is banal and pretentious.

It displaces the traditional popular culture which is more directly and experientially connected to the social condition of the working classes — those who produce and consume it.

The study of culture was thus the study of the ways and means by which the mass media and imported American culture were "colonizing" the working classes.

While the task of cultural studies was **value analysis**, its goal was **value judgement**.

aymond Williams

Raymond Williams also started his academic career as an adult education tutor – he taught at Oxford University from 1946 to 1960. His books *Culture and Society* (1958) and *The Long Revolution* (1961) draw on two traditions within Marxism.

These are the <u>practice</u> of seeing culture as specific expressions of the coherence of organic communities and <u>resisting</u> determinism in its various forms.

Raymond Williams

For Williams, culture is an all-inclusive entity, a "whole way of life, material, intellectual and spiritual". He traces the evolution of culture through its various historical conditions towards a "complete" form. Williams sees the emergence of a "general human culture" in specific societies where it is shaped by local and temporary systems.

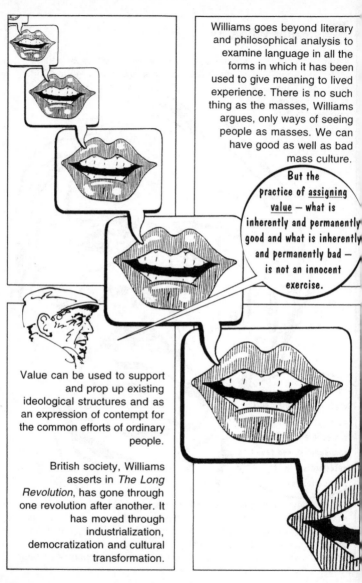

Williams goes beyond literary and philosophical analysis to examine language in all the forms in which it has been used to give meaning to lived experience. There is no such thing as the masses, Williams argues, only ways of seeing people as masses. We can have good as well as bad mass culture.

But the practice of assigning value — what is inherently and permanently good and what is inherently and permanently bad — is not an innocent exercise.

Value can be used to support and prop up existing ideological structures and as an expression of contempt for the common efforts of ordinary people.

British society, Williams asserts in *The Long Revolution*, has gone through one revolution after another. It has moved through industrialization, democratization and cultural transformation.

E.P. Thompson: Understanding Class

A dedicated peace campaigner and Vice-President of the Campaign for Nuclear Disarmament (CND), E.P. Thompson was a radical historian who changed the perception of British history. In his seminal work, *The Making of the English Working Class* (1978), he sought to demonstrate the coming-into-being of the English working class in a specific historical period and thereby to recover the agency, concerns and experience of the mass of the English population ignored by the dominant tradition of conventional history.

My main difference with theoretical Marxists and sociologists is my insistence that class is an historical phenomenon that cannot be understood as a <u>structure</u> or a <u>category</u>.

Class is not a thing – it is something which in fact happens (and can be shown to have happened) in human relationships.

Remembering History

To understand class, Thompson argues, it is essential to see it "as a social and cultural formation arising from processes which can only be studied as they work themselves out over a considerable historical period".

It is not that working-class culture has different sources from "high" culture, though it does create whole new areas of distinct cultural engagement, association and creative activity.

Thompson demonstrates the difference in meaning that shared sources could have. For example, John Bunyan's classic allegory *Pilgrim's Progress* (1678, 1684) and the 18th century religious movement of Methodism cross-cut English society. The significance is in the different ways in which they enable, say, a mechanic to arrive at consciousness of his position vis-à-vis a Duchess and to engage in activity designed to *change* that relationship.

Culture must be understood through the experiences and contributions of the winners and losers. We cannot impose judgements where "only the successful are remembered", while "the blind alleys, the lost causes, and the losers themselves are forgotten".

The vibrancy and meaning of culture are as much in evidence among the casualties and victims as the supposed winners.

The possible developments of cultural studies that lead from Thompson's work are considerable. Popular mass culture is not a new creation of consumer society – it has *history*. Moreover, Thompson's distinction between a culture made *for* the working class, rather than *by* the working class, is important. At a time when meanings are being sought for periods of less than a decade, Thompson's emphasis on meaningful social change "over a considerable historical period" should help us to distinguish the significant from the trivial.

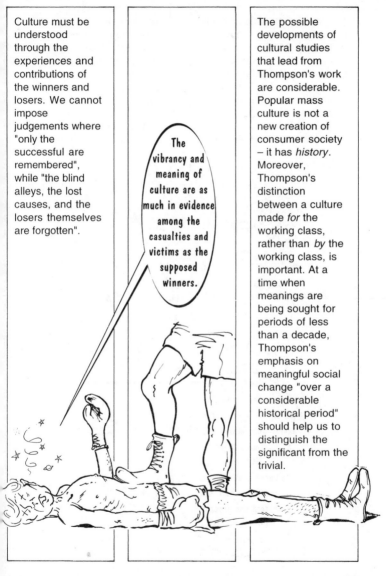

Thompson took issue with the French philosopher **Louis Althusser** (1918-90) who introduced the fashion for structuralism into Marxism (see page 44). His trenchant counterblast to Althusserian Marxism, published as *The Poverty of Theory* (1978), made him an ambiguous figure for many practitioners of cultural studies.

Yet, there is a consistent, reasoned and principled sanity in all his acerbic engagements and arguments. Certainly, his assertion that "causes which were lost in England might, in Asia or Africa, yet be won" offers us a vision of plurality and openness that is worth following.

History is a form within which we fight, and many have fought before us. For the past is not just dead, inert, confining; it carries signs and evidences also of creative resources which can sustain the present and prefigure possibility!

Merde!

Stuart Hall

Stuart Hall, sociologist and critic, is perhaps the most canonized of the founding fathers. Indeed, as one critic has noted, cultural studies has tended falsely to unify itself around a small number of highly problematic articles by Stuart Hall. He was born in Jamaica ("early 1930s") into a middle class and conservative family. In 1951, Hall won a scholarship to Oxford – and the rest, as they say, is (cultural) history.

In the 1950s, Hall was a leading light of the New Left; in the 1960s and 70s, he was at the Centre for Contemporary Cultural Studies, Birmingham; in the 1980s, he moved to the Open University and led the "New Times" debate at *Marxism Today*.

Intellectual Practice

Hall has always been involved in activism *and* theoretical work. He believes that cultural studies needs to hold both theoretical and political questions "in an ever irresolvable, but permanent tension", allowing one "to irritate and bother and disturb the other". It is important to Hall that the tension remains.

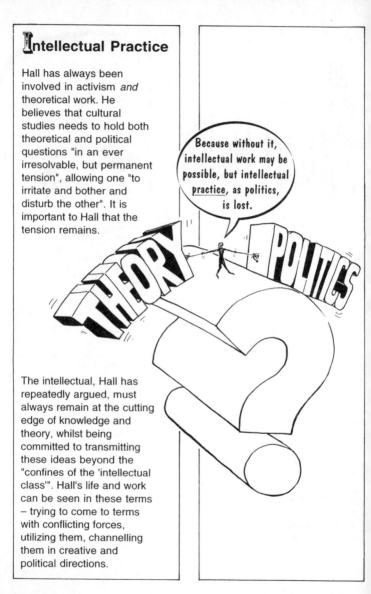

Because without it, intellectual work may be possible, but intellectual <u>practice</u>, as politics, is lost.

THEORY

POLITICS

The intellectual, Hall has repeatedly argued, must always remain at the cutting edge of knowledge and theory, whilst being committed to transmitting these ideas beyond the "confines of the 'intellectual class'". Hall's life and work can be seen in these terms – trying to come to terms with conflicting forces, utilizing them, channelling them in creative and political directions.

Culture Makes a Difference

Hall has described himself as always remaining within "shouting distance of Marx". However, in the late 1950s and early 60s, he rejected Marxism in favour of "an urgent sense of engaging with the contemporary". This changed in the 1970s when Marx was hauled back: "We chose as a coherent theory … not previously analysed, that of Karl Marx." During this period, the Centre focused on "structural Marxism". In the early 1980s, Hall was writing about a "Marxism without guarantees". In the late 1980s and early 90s, the "Marxist element" was "more or less abandoned".

However, despite his ambiguous relationship with Marxism, Hall has never accepted that the class struggle explains and determines everything.

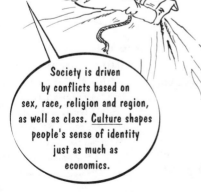

Society is driven by conflicts based on sex, race, religion and region, as well as class. <u>Culture</u> shapes people's sense of identity just as much as economics.

Stuart Hall has always insisted that cultural studies can actually have a practical impact on reality. He challenges intellectuals by asking: "what real effect are you making on the world?"

The answer to this question will determine what cultural studies "can do, can't, can never do; but also, what it has to do, what it alone has a privileged capacity to do".

Against the urgency of people dying in the streets, what in God's name is the point of cultural studies?

What is the point of the study of representations, if there is no response to the question of what you say to someone who wants to know if they should take a drug for AIDS, and if that means they'll die two days later or a few months earlier?

During its formative phase, British cultural studies was deeply influenced by the New Left. Indeed, the formation and development of the New Left is seen by many historians as a precursor to cultural studies. The New Left emerged as a British response to the Russian invasion of Hungary in 1956.

Stalin's brutal suppression of a popular uprising in the "Soviet bloc" nation of Hungary became a defining event for Western European Communism.

Many of those who denounced the Stalinist variety of Marxism formed the New Left.

Students and intellectuals from former British colonies, who moved on the fringes and were never allowed to be part of the dominant institutions of the British left, played a key role in the formation of the New Left.

The Internationalism of Cultural Studies

Indeed, the New Left emerged largely because it was almost impossible for non-English intellectuals to break into the British left establishment. According to Stuart Hall, this is a critical point in understanding the history of both the New Left and British cultural studies.

Colonial intellectuals not only challenged the "Britishness" of the New Left, but also stressed the part played by "outside" forces which these colonial intellectuals represented.

"Outsiders" would not have been in Britain without a long history of colonial relations.

We came to our colonial "homeland" to study, and thus introduced external voices and perspectives on the conventional positions of the left.

Without colonial intellectuals, there would be no British New Left; and perhaps no cultural studies. Thus, right from its beginning, British cultural studies is more than British – rather, it is *internationalist*.

Broadening the Issues

But the concerns of colonial intellectuals did not enter British cultural studies until the 1980s. In the 70s, British cultural studies became obsessed with the "style" and behaviour of young working-class men.

The behaviour of such groups as mods, rockers and punks was seen as presenting symbolic resistance to the dominant system.

The "styles" of their dress, hair-dos, music and dance-hall rituals were "read" and "interrogated" for symbols of resistance.

The narrow perspective of cultural studies in Britain was only broadened in the 1980s to include women and blacks in a class-ridden and racially divided society.

During the Thatcher period, when privatization and free market policies became the norm, subcultures and subgroups of women and minorities became the focus of cultural analysis seeking to expose the impact of "liberalization" on the marginalized elements of society. As before, the emphasis was on "reading" signs of resistance and opposition to the dominant culture.

British cultural studies has two distinguishing features. First: it is distinguished by the remarkable diversity and originality of the topics that have been studied. Apart from the studies of youth subcultures and television news programmes …

British cultural studies has focused on images of women, masculinity and the history of sexuality.

It has examined how the past is presented in museums.

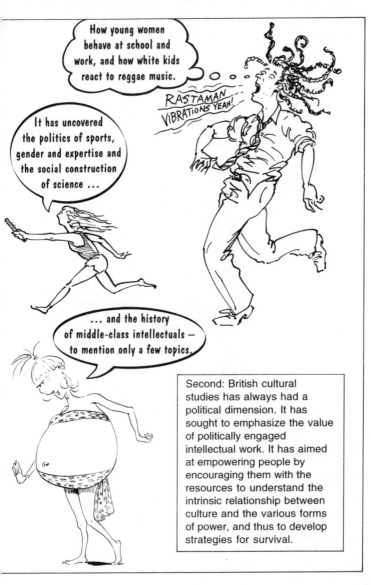

How young women behave at school and work, and how white kids react to reggae music.

RASTAMAN VIBRATIONS YEAH!

It has uncovered the politics of sports, gender and expertise and the social construction of science ...

... and the history of middle-class intellectuals — to mention only a few topics.

Second: British cultural studies has always had a political dimension. It has sought to emphasize the value of politically engaged intellectual work. It has aimed at empowering people by encouraging them with the resources to understand the intrinsic relationship between culture and the various forms of power, and thus to develop strategies for survival.

Althusser's Structuralism

The French philosopher **Louis Althusser** (1918-90) imported structuralism into Marxism in his effort to make it a "science". Althusser conceptualizes society as a *structured whole* which consists of relatively autonomous levels – legal, political, cultural – whose mode of articulation (or "effectivity", as he says) is only determined "in the last instance" by the economy. What matter are the *differences* between the levels and not the apparent "mirror" role that each element plays in expressing the identity of the whole.

Structuralism has two crucial aspects. First, the recognition that **differential relations** are the key to understanding culture and society. Second, as a result, structure is not prior to the realization of these relations.

So, for scientific Marxism, there is no "society" but only *modes of production* which evolve in history and are permanently inherent in the relatively autonomous levels of the structured whole.

44

Marxist "science" rejects the idea of a universal "human nature" and embraces "theoretical anti-humanism". This eliminates the individual as in any sense a conscious actor in producing social relations. Individuals are not prior to social conditions. Each subject is an agent of the system.

Sigmund Freud
1856–1939

Althusser borrowed the term "overdetermined" from me to signal that the reality of the economic level (mode of production) is not expressed in ideology or in consciousness but exists in a **displaced form** throughout the social formation.

There is not one but many (over) determinants — economic, political and cultural — competing with and contradicting each other to create a "society".

Althusserian analysis was absorbed by British cultural studies in the 1970s. Here are three key ideas. The main ideological instruments of society – law, religion, education, family – are just as important as economic conditions. Culture is neither totally dependent on nor totally independent of economic conditions and relationships. Ideology does not construct "false consciousness" as traditional Marxists had always argued.

Ideology provides a conceptual framework through which we interpret and make sense of our lived, material conditions.

Ideology therefore produces our culture, as well as our consciousness of who and what we are.

Althusserian terminology – "problematic", "overdetermined" and so on – is evident in the Birmingham centre's journal of cultural studies. But there was always unease with Althusser. Stuart Hall tended to deny using him. E.P. Thompson monumentally attacked Althusser's anti-humanism and denial of individual action as ideas deeply repugnant to a militant historian of the working class (in *The Poverty of Theory*, 1978).

I've wrestled with Althusser. But my real hero is Antonio Gramsci.

And he certainly **should** be!

Let's now see why Gramsci would be more appealing than Althusser.

The Influence of Antonio Gramsci

Antonio Gramsci (1891-1937), political activist, Marxist philosopher and a founder of the Italian Communist Party, believed that Lenin's Bolshevik revolution in Russia (1917) could be transplanted to Italy. He thought the Factory Council movement in Turin and Piedmont could translate the experience of the Russian Soviets and empower the industrial working class as a revolutionary force. A general strike in 1920 was followed by the occupation of the factories throughout Northern Italy. In fact, this ended in defeat when the government replaced striking workers with Southern peasants.

Hegemony

Despite his immunity as an elected member of parliament, Gramsci was arrested by the Fascists in 1926 and spent the rest of his life in prison. He had the misfortune of "enforced leisure" to reflect on the socialist defeat and the crucial role of culture in society.

The key term in Gramsci's thought is **hegemony**, which is critical for an understanding of history and the structure of any given society. Hegemony is what binds society together without the use of force.

> This is achieved when the upper classes supplement their economic power by creating "intellectual and moral leadership".

To achieve this leadership, compromises are made with the working classes and a general consent is generated. Gramsci saw this process as the key to the success of liberal democracies in Britain and France. Both *negotiation* and *consent* are essential terms for understanding hegemony. Ideas, values and beliefs are not imposed from above, neither do they develop in a free and accidental way, but are negotiated through a whole series of encounters and collisions between classes.

> This active process, which operates on a number of fronts, eventually leads to a "compromise equilibrium" between competing classes.

Culture is one of the key sites where struggle for hegemony takes place; and it is in the arena of *popular* culture that the issues of "moral and intellectual leadership" are resolved.

Intellectuals

Intellectuals also play a key role in Gramsci's ideas. The common notion of intellectuals is that of a small élite group of highly intelligent, morally endowed, independent men (always) who constitute the conscience of mankind (sic).

> Against this, I argue that <u>all men are intellectuals</u>. But not all men have in society the function of intellectuals.

Gramsci favoured "organic intellectuals", those who openly identified with an oppressed class, shared its interests and worked on its behalf.

Gramsci's ideas have suffered from partial and partisan misinterpretation over the years. A series of movements, groups and individuals have absorbed and manipulated his theories – cultural studies being just one example. In cultural studies, "hegemony theory" does not operate as Gramsci originally formulated it.

> We've expanded it beyond the boundaries of class power and relations to include issues of race and gender, culture and consumerism, meaning and pleasure.

> Fine! That agrees with my idea of the "subaltern" (see page 79).

Throughout the history of cultural studies, Gramsci has been used to expose the hegemonic tendencies of a wide variety of cultural, intellectual and philosophical positions.

Criticism of British Cultural Studies

British cultural studies has been strongly criticized for its parochialism and "Anglocentrism", its over-emphasis on class at the expense of race and gender, and its over concern with and romantic treatment of urban style and subcultural rituals.

"Culture" in British cultural studies has often been represented as "*the* culture".

British popular culture is projected as a prototype model for the world to follow.

British cultural studies speaks from the metropolitan centres of Birmingham and London — locations where the concerns and perspectives of the margins are seldom considered.

British cultural studies speaks about working classes, women, blacks and other minorities, but its practitioners are overwhelmingly white, middle-class and male.

The notion of "art" in British cultural studies is also seen as particularly Eurocentric. Only Western culture views the arts as a source of meaning through which life is recreated in all its dimensions. The idea that every self-conscious individual life aspires to the condition of art is not endorsed by non-Western cultures.

Despite its declared aim to be the champion of the marginalized and disempowered, cultural studies maintained a continuing relationship with the supremacist Western "culture and civilization" tradition of the colonial and post-colonial period.

British cultural studies has also glorified certain popular art forms as cultural archetypes.

The music video, for example, has been over-analysed. So many readings of these texts are trite and banal.

Similarly, British television practice, particularly Channel 4 productions, are championed as representations of "the people" and "minorities" – a perspective that, while insisting on maintaining difference, actually dissolves it by assuming commonality across cultures and social structures.

British cultural studies has also been accused of being Marxism in disguise – "a 'cover' for a revised and qualified Marxism". This criticism is justified in the sense that Marxism has influenced cultural studies in two specific ways. **First**, the assumption of cultural studies that industrial capitalist societies are unequally divided along class, gender and ethnic lines is drawn from Marxism. But cultural studies goes further in contending that culture is the main arena where this division is established and fought for, where subordinate and marginalized groups resist the imposition of meanings which reflect the interests of the dominant groups.

This is what makes culture in general, and cultural studies in particular, an <u>ideological</u> enterprise.

Second, cultural studies has accepted and accommodated, some critics claim, the Marxist materialist notion of history. Certainly, cultural studies attempts to analyse social structures in terms of how cultural forces have given them an *historic* form. The reason culture is important is that it shapes history as well as social structures. Hence, cultural studies does not treat history and culture as separate entities. However, on the whole, cultural studies has tended to oppose reductionist Marxism, understood as a hard determinism of both history and economics.

The Migration of Cultural Studies

During the Thatcher years (1979-90), British cultural studies began to fragment and leave the shores of Britain. Cultural studies migrated to the United States, Canada, Australia, France and India.

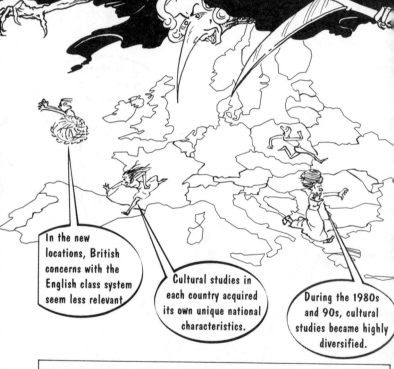

In the new locations, British concerns with the English class system seem less relevant.

Cultural studies in each country acquired its own unique national characteristics.

During the 1980s and 90s, cultural studies became highly diversified.

In certain locations, it became less political and more concerned with aesthetic and textual analysis. In other regions, it became more political and involved with the plight of the marginalized and discourses of the periphery. Let's see where and why these differences occurred.

American Cultural Studies

Cultural studies crossed the Atlantic in the mid-1980s, a period when the humanities as a whole were in some turmoil and undergoing a sociological transformation in the United States. Many disciplines were moving towards a more active engagement with the politics of social identity and an examination of the representations of cultural forms.

In media studies, for example, emphasis was shifting towards the ethnography of audiences.

There was also a minority tradition of communication studies, over a decade old, which argued for interpreting communication as a way of creating and transforming a shared culture.

Media texts were being examined for their roles in creating popular cultural formations.

It was, therefore, not too difficult for cultural studies to be rapidly adopted and absorbed in the US academic institutional structure.

As cultural studies became institutionalized in the US, it also rapidly became professionalized. It quickly acquired its own technical language – drawn largely from semiotics and literary theory – and, despite its original anti-discipline credentials, it was transformed into a discipline. From being an intellectual tradition, cultural studies in America became an organized professional activity in the broad area of liberal scholarship.

The relative absence of a left intellectual tradition further isolated cultural studies in America from its British political roots. It became the preserve of scholars who hardly had any direct connection with existing political and cultural movements.

On the whole, we did not consider the link between cultural studies and political action as important or even desirable.

Questions of power and politics, class and intellectual formation, so fundamental to the British exponents of cultural studies, lost their significance in the United States.

Hardly surprising, then, that cultural studies in the US lost many of its Marxist assumptions – not least because Marxism came under severe attack from the postmodernists. The French philosopher **Jean-François Lyotard** (b. 1924) introduced the essential postmodern idea of "incredulity towards Grand Narratives" in his seminal book **The Postmodern Condition** (1979).

Following Lyotard, postmodernists identify Marxism as a continuation of the Enlightenment project.

We take issue with its status as a teleological and fundamental theory, a "Grand Narrative" of liberation.

As well as its essentialism, deterministic economics and its Eurocentrism.

The collapse of communism in the Soviet Union and the Eastern "bloc" countries in 1989, with the consequent discrediting of socialism, further distanced American cultural studies from critical Marxism.

Again, it is not surprising that American cultural studies has come under severe criticism, both from the British pioneers in the field and from those – uncharitably described as puritans – who would like to duplicate the formative history of cultural studies in other parts of the world. The strongest criticism of American cultural studies dismisses it as a generalized form of textual analysis and free-floating theorization.

It has developed an esoteric framework far removed from the more generous boundaries of cultural studies in Britain.

Under the influence of postmodernism, the significance of culture as practice, form and institution has evaporated.

I don't know what to say about American cultural studies. I am completely dumbfounded by it.

KULCHA

Canadian Cultural Studies

Cultural studies arrived in Canada about the same time as it did in the United States, and settled in about the same place: in departments of communication studies. But communication studies in Canada always had different concerns from those in the US, and reflected specifically Canadian issues. Cultural studies in Canada focuses on what is broadly described as the "Canadian experience". Canada has several particular and peculiar features.

We share the longest border in the world with the United States.

We have a relatively small population (smaller than the state of California).

And there are at least three groups — the English-speaking, French-speaking and indigenous minorities — competing for power and attention.

Canadian cultural studies is thus concerned primarily with the questions and issues of Canadian **nationality**.

How can people of such diverse backgrounds, living across such a vast and underpopulated territory, be transformed into a coherent nation?

How can the Canadian culture(s) resist the permanent onslaught from the southern border?

What would ensure the individuality of the Canadian experience in the face of films, televisio music and other media and cultural consumer products emanating from the US?

Canadian cultural studies is therefore focused on investigations of its own self-definition.

Australian Cultural Studies

Intellectual tradition in Australia has always tended to be influenced by the British. True to this intellectual history, Australian cultural studies has absorbed most of the historic elements of British cultural studies. Indeed, as more than one critic has noticed, cultural studies in Australia produces "ironic echoes" of the "original map of British imperialism's conquest" with an "inordinate number of left academics wandering round Australia, but talking about Birmingham".

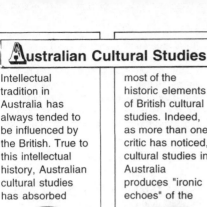

Cultural studies was embraced by critical and nationalist movements within literary studies in Australia.

It also found desirable residence in departments of film and media studies, as well as in the resourceful and multi-disciplinary field of Australian studies.

All of these disciplines were concerned with identifying distinctive features of Australian life.

The evolution of cultural studies in Australia was particularly influenced by the decision of the government to bankroll the Australian film industry – a decision which directly led to the revival of Australian films in the 1970s. State-funding bodies, which singularly determined the character of Australian films, saw films not so much as a commercial enterprise but more as a vehicle for representing the nation at home and abroad.

Films which presented the nation in a less than favourable way were shunned.

The revived film industry thus championed an official, conservative definition of Australian culture by concentrating on costume drama and films that glorified European colonial history.

Also suppressed were local genres such as the radical nationalist "ocker films".

Australian cultural studies has sought to interrogate the whole notion of "the national character" in film, history and literary theory by focusing on local texts, institutions and discourses. However, while it acknowledges that the Australian identity makes sense only when analysed in terms of nation, and cannot be seen in terms of class or as a subculture of Britain, it nevertheless draws its main theoretical and analytical categories from British cultural studies.

It is only in the set of questions that it asks in relation to the national identity that Australian cultural studies differs from British cultural studies.

Mad Max: a national Australian hero?

French Cultural Studies

France went through a radical transformation during the 1960s. A major change was brought about by decolonization. In Vietnam, the French were driven out by the military successes of the Viet Minh. In North Africa, eight years of brutal war in Algeria led to its independence from France in 1962. The famous student unrest of 1968 further radicalized French politics.

THE IDEA IS NOT TO PUT POETRY AT THE SERVICE OF THE REVOLUTION . . .

. . . BUT TO PUT THE REVOLUTION AT THE SERVICE OF POETRY

Decolonization posed the question "what is France?"

Social changes raised the question "who is French?"

French cultural studies has been largely concerned with these two fundamental questions.

To understand the complexity of the question "what is France?", one needs to appreciate the north-south divide within France. Certain areas – like Corsica, Brittany and the Eastern Provinces – have been in and out of France over periods of time.

This affects how we in these regions see France and ourselves.

WE WILL NOT LEAD. WE WILL ONLY DETONATE.

The hegemony of Paris over other parts of France produces further tension in the regions.

Who is French is even more problematic. Immigrants from Eastern, Central and Mediterranean Europe, and more recently from North Africa, have totally transformed the ethnic mix of France. There are big French-speaking communities in other countries such as Belgium and Switzerland, and in North Africa (and other parts of Africa).

A major question for French cultural studies is whether cultural knowledge (e.g. command of language) is the essential basis of being French.

Initially, France followed a policy of **assimilation** — the ultimate aim being to raise the cultural level of the immigrants to that of the French, thus assimilating them into "the nation".

This policy failed and was replaced with the theory of *association*. This amounted to a new school syllabus giving more recognition to the cultures and homelands of the immigrants. But the general idea that French culture was superior remained.

CHEB HASNI

KHALED

CHEIKHA

THE QUEEN OF RAÏ MUSIC

The Beurs, French nationals of African origins who identify themselves by their cultural difference, pose a particular problem for French identity. Beurs have made a strong cultural impact on France, particularly with their unique music, a blend of Algerian traditional music with rock.

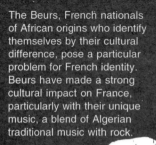

AÏT BU
GUEMMEZ

The Beur movement began in the 1970s when we young North Africans started forming theatre groups.

Our plays were in French, with some Arabic, and depicted our everyday struggles with poverty, racism and cultural contradictions.

LES GNAWAS

But are French-African cultures part of French cultural studies?

Some theorists have argued that colonial experience means that the former French colonies *do* share a unique cultural relationship with France, and that French-African culture is a legitimate part of French cultural studies. But the inclusion of African culture in French cultural studies raises the question: how generalized is the French-African experience? Aren't there several ethnic groupings, subcultures and classes within the "African experience"?

DON CHERRY

69

French identity is also shaped by external Others. For a long time, France's primary Other was Germany. Since 1945, its Other has been the United States with its powerful cultural and economic influence. The Americanization of France has become a major issue for French cultural studies.

American ideas and consumer culture are replacing the "norms" of French culture. People are robbed of their language and turned into passive subjects of a foreign power.

We see American cinema as a "Trojan Horse" and Euro-Disney as "culture Chernobyl"

Asterix the Gaul, the "wisecracking warrior" who battles the Romans, triumphs, and celebrates a sense of community, was published as a response to the hegemony of American comics.

The thorny questions of what France is (the nation), who the French are (the people) and the divisions in French society (gender, geography, race, class) are fault-lines that give French cultural studies its peculiar vitality. It is almost as if France thrives in adversity.

ierre Bourdieu

Pierre Bourdieu (b. 1930), sociologist and educationalist, is one of the most prominent exponents of French cultural studies. In a string of books, he has painstakingly shown the complex and intrinsic relationship between the struggle for social power and the use of cultural products by different social groups. Bourdieu starts by asking: who consumes what kind of culture? And what effect does this consumption have? In *L'Amour de l'art: Les Musées d'art Européens et leur public* (1966) Bourdieu and his collaborator, Alain Darbel, show that the visitors to state-run art galleries are divided along class and educational lines.

> On the whole, working-class people do not visit art galleries and they particularly shun modern art.

> We think of art galleries as churches, rather than, say, a library or a shop.

> We experience antagonism and alienation and stay for a much shorter time than middle- and upper-class visitors.

Art galleries serve the cultivated, privileged class; and this privilege is legitimized by claiming a distinction between "good" and vulgar taste, legitimate and illegitimate styles.

Aesthetic judgements, Bourdieu shows, do not follow some kind of objective, autonomous aesthetic logic – rather, they substitute distinctions of taste for class distinctions and therefore fortify the divisions between classes and assert the right of the ruling class to sanction their authority over other classes. Bourdieu uses an economic metaphor to make this point.

"Cultural capital" is the ability to read and understand cultural codes; but this ability, and hence "cultural capital", is not distributed equally amongst social classes.

It's a dirty statue and no mistake.

The working classes have little "cultural capital" and systematically lose out in the battle for cultural power. When "cultural capital" is invested in the exercise of taste, it yields both high profit for those who possess it and a "profit in legitimacy" which is the justification of the ruling class to be the ruling class, to be what it is "right" to be.

Bourdieu argues this point in *Distinction* (1980).

Ah, yes! I see its artistic worth.

A work of art has interest and meaning only for those who possess "cultural capital" and can read the codes into which it is encoded.

South Asian Cultural Studies

Nowhere outside the US is cultural studies thriving more than in South Asia. Indeed, if **Vinay Lal**'s (b. 1961) extensive bibliography of *South Asian Cultural Studies* (1996) is anything to go by, one can be forgiven for thinking that, like cricket...

...cultural studies is an Indian invention accidentally discovered by the British.

South Asian cultural studies evolved through cultural studies of science. During the 1970s, such major works as Jit Singh Uberoi's *Science and Culture* (1978), Claude Alvares' *Homo Faber: Technology and Culture in India, China and the West* (1979) and Ashis Nandy's *Alternative Sciences* (1980) laid the foundation for a sustained critique of modernity and the pathology of rationality in Western science. By the early 1980s new work from the Bombay-based Patriotic People's Science and Technology Group and from writers like Deepak Kumar, Shiv Visvanathan and Veena Das had ensured that radical scholarship in India was "guided by the belief that all knowledge is political intervention".

Tamil

Kotas (Nilgiri Hills)

Malabar (Tiyan caste)

The CSDS

There are three distinct (and often warring!) schools of South Asian cultural studies.

The scholars at the Centre for the Study of Developing Societies (CSDS), Delhi, established in 1963, practise a special model of cultural studies rooted in indigenous forms of social knowledge. The theoretical work of Rajni Kothari, Ashis Nandy and D.L. Sheth, amongst others, has problematized the idea of culture and questioned the standardized categories of politics, economics and science.

CSDS scholars are largely concerned with three main issues. The first relates to the experience of transformation of "pre-modern" communities into modern collectives.

Rajput

Lepcha

Brahmin fakir

These empirical and theoretical studies in ethnicity, religion and gender may be described as attempts to capture the momentary contacts of history with ahistorical structures.

Bhil

Hindu (Benares)

Bengali

The second is concerned with the conversation of cultures. Here, "incomprehension" is sometimes used as a theoretically provocative method to study the making of cultures.

A culture is seen to preserve its inner strength not only by conversing with others but by remaining fully incommunicado.

Lepcha (Sikkim)

Sikh

The third involves the recovery of cultures of the politically marginalized by the state and the hegemonic ideologies of nationalism, secularism, scientific temper, rationality and cultural universalism.

Here, the focus is on the mechanism of marginalization and the tactics adopted by dissident cultures to defy their predicament.

Kling

Parsee

Hindu (Calcutta)

CCS or the "Teen Murti"

A heterogeneous group of scholars based at The Centre of Contemporary Studies (CCS) at the Nehru Memorial Museum and Library (also known as "Teen Murti"), Delhi, practise a more conventional form of cultural studies. Scholars like R.S. Rajan and Geeta Kumar are as concerned with film, dance and street culture as with Indian English and global domination. Perhaps the most renowned amongst them is Aijaz Ahmad, Marxist scholar and translator of the *ghazals* of the classical Urdu poet **Ghalib** (1797-1869).

Ghalib

The Subaltern Studies Collective

The Subaltern Studies collective is based around Delhi University. Their main organ is the annual journal *Subaltern Studies: Writings on South Asian History and Society*, first published in 1982. The term "subaltern" is drawn from Gramsci's paper, "On the Margins of History: history of the subaltern social group" (1934).

I first used "subaltern" as a collective description for a variety of different dominated and exploited groups who explicitly lack class-consciousness.

In the work of the Subaltern Studies group, we use the term to describe the peasants, the insurgents who periodically rose up against the British colonialists, or, more generally, "the people".

The subalterns represent the demographic difference between the total Indian population and all those who could be described as the élite.

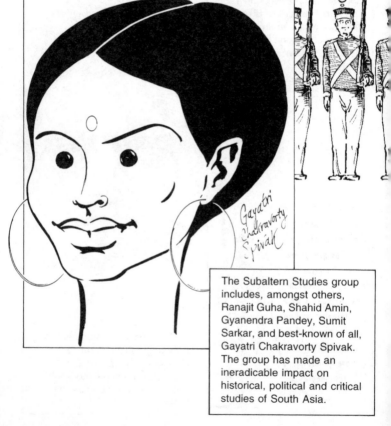

Subaltern Studies is basically a school of Indian colonial history. Its main concern is to unearth, investigate and describe the contribution made by the people on their own, independently of the élite, and to establish a subaltern or peasant consciousness.

Our work reclaims history and offers a theory of consciousness and change where the agency of change is firmly located in the insurgent or the subaltern.

insurgent?

Gayatri Chakravorty Spivak

The Subaltern Studies group includes, amongst others, Ranajit Guha, Shahid Amin, Gyanendra Pandey, Sumit Sarkar, and best-known of all, Gayatri Chakravorty Spivak. The group has made an ineradicable impact on historical, political and critical studies of South Asia.

(*It's all lies! It's all lies!)

The Influence of Gandhi

South Asian cultural studies has two other important features. The first concerns the influence of **M.K. Gandhi** (1869-1948), the founder of modern independent India, on Indian culture and his reinterpretation as a "Green" leader. The impact of Gandhian thinking on ecology has produced a strong grass-roots ecological movement in India.

We peasants and villagers have been a driving force both in the critiques of development ...

... and in attempts to discover a more humane and viable relationship between humans and nature.

South Asian cultural studies has tackled these issues head-on, as can be seen in the work of Vandana Shiva and Tariq Benuri.

The Place of English

The second concerns the role and place of English in India. To what extent can we describe English as the language of the people?

How does English exist politically in relation to Indian languages?

What association does English have with structure of class and caste?

How does English do the work of hegemony in India?

What are the particular features of Indian English?

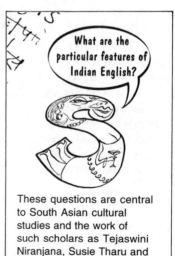

These questions are central to South Asian cultural studies and the work of such scholars as Tejaswini Niranjana, Susie Tharu and Rajeswari Sunder Rajan.

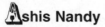shis Nandy

Ashis Nandy (b. 1937), psychologist and cultural critic, can be described as the father of South Asian cultural studies. His main concern is to make cultural studies a totally indigenous enterprise based on the Subcontinent's unique categories of knowing and being. Nandy categorically locates himself with the victims of history and the casualties of an array of grand Western ideas, such as Science, Rationality, Development and the Nation State.

Nandy seeks both to unite the victims and to increase the awareness of their victimhood.

Here are a few of Nandy's ideas. First, on **colonialism** ...

What the European imperial powers did in the colonies bounced back to the fatherland as a new political and public culture. Colonialism transformed Britain culturally by suppressing and declaring tenderness, speculation and introspection as feminine and therefore unworthy of public culture, and by bringing the most brutish and masculine elements of British colonial life to the fore.

The Stereotyped Oriental

Colonialism *replaced* the Eurocentric convention of portraying the Other as an incomprehensible barbarian with the pathological stereotype of the strange but predictable Oriental. He was now religious but superstitious, clever but devious, chaotically violent but effeminately cowardly. At the same time, a new discourse was developed where the basic mode of breaking out of these stereotypes was to reverse them: superstitious but spiritual, uneducated but wise, womanly but pacific.

No colonialism could be complete unless it "universalized" and enriched its ethnic stereotypes by appropriating the language of defiance of its victims.

Little dear... (such a shame you'll grow up into a superstitious, spiritual, uneducated, wise, womanly, pacific Oriental...)

The cry of the victims of colonialism was ultimately the cry to be heard in another language -- which would be unknown both to the colonizer and the anti-colonial movements that he had bred and domesticated.

The Permeable Self

Traditional societies have an ability to live with cultural ambiguities and to use them to build psychological and even metaphysical defences against cultural invasions.

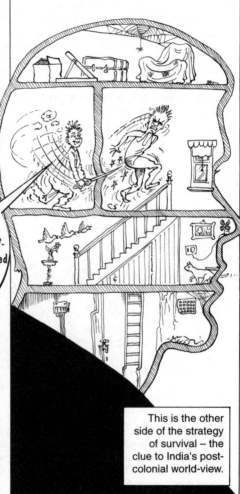

Traditional culture demands that a certain permeability of boundaries be maintained in one's self-image. The self is not defined too tightly or separated mechanically from the not-self.

This is the other side of the strategy of survival – the clue to India's post-colonial world-view.

The Non-Player and the Future

Dissent has been domesticated. All resistance to and dissent from hegemonic impulses falls into two categories: violence or pacifism. Nandy posits a third way – the dissenter as *non-player*. The non-player plays another game altogether, a game of dissenting visions and futures. The future itself is a state of awareness. And the main aim of the game is to transform the future by changing human awareness of the future. By defining what is "immutable" and "universal", the West silences the visions of Other cultures to ensure the continuity of its own linear projections of the past and the present on to the future.

By avoiding thinking about the future, Other cultures become prisoners of the past, present and the future of Western civilization.

I'M NOT PLAYING

To break out of this structure, Nandy contends, non-Western cultures must define their own future in terms of their own categories and concepts, articulating their visions in language that is true to their own Self, even if not comprehensible "on the other side of the global fence of academic respectability".

What is the Solution?

Finally, what are the possible boundaries of a solution?

> Our release from institutionalized suffering must involve both the non-West as well as the West.

But this is not an invitation for the masculine, oppressive West to transform itself; it is to recognize that the oppressed and marginalized Selves in the West need help and can be used as allies in civilization's battle against institutionalized suffering.

> It is the non-Western civilizations that must give collective representation to all suffering everywhere — the suffering of the past as well as the present — to release the bondage of suffering in the future.

The non-Western civilizations have to be aware of both the outside forces of cruelty and grief, as well as the "inner vectors" that have dislodged their true Selves. They have to do more than simply resist the West: they have to transform their cultures into cultures of resistance.

Cultural Studies of Science

This area of cultural studies is the most ideologically sensitive of all, for science has been, and still is, the totem of European secular culture. In the centuries-long struggle between the ideologues of science and those of religion, the central claim was that science uniquely had truth, as opposed to nonsense studies like theology and metaphysics.

This exclusive claim derives its plausibility from the obvious successes of science in transforming human knowledge and humanity's material conditions.

It's a stereotypical scientist!

But your philosophical arguments are based on the supposedly "objective" and "value-free" nature of scientific knowledge.

Ironically, "value-freedom" is a false-consciousness of the same sort that scientistic philosophers ascribe to those holding other belief systems.

The practice of science, as with any form of disciplined study, is profoundly shaped by value commitments.

Values enter science in a number of ways. The first point of entry is the selection of the problem to be investigated – the *choice* of the problem, *who* makes the choice and on *what* grounds. Society, the political realities of power, prejudice and value systems will influence even the "purest" science.

Often, it is the source of funding that defines what problem is to be investigated.

If funding comes from government sources, then it will reflect the priorities of the government — whether space exploration is more important than the health problems of the inner city poor.

Or whether nuclear power should be developed rather than solar energy.

Spare change?

Values also play an important part in determining what is actually seen as a problem, what questions are asked and how they are answered. For example, cancer rather than diabetes may be seen as a problem, even though they may both claim the same number of victims. Here both political and ideological concerns can make one problem invisible while focusing attention on another.

In his classic study *Scientific Knowledge and its Social Problems* (1971), **Jerome Revetz** (b. 1929) made most of these points. Other critics such as Hilary and Steven Rose reinforced the arguments. But behind these analyses there was a long story of demystification of science which involved fierce battles in philosophy and the history of science.

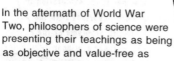

In the aftermath of World War Two, philosophers of science were presenting their teachings as being as objective and value-free as science itself, when in fact they were descended from the committed, even militant "logical positivists" of the 1920s Vienna Circle.

The essence of science can be rescued by replacing a "logic of confirmation" with an ethical principle of self-criticism.

Karl Popper (1902-94)

This insight was very powerful for human action in general, particularly politics, when applied by Popper in his book *The Open Society and its Enemies* (1945), and it made him enormously influential. But when he tried to embody this in the scientific logic of refutations, he encountered insoluble difficulties.

The real revolution in the philosophy of science – introducing the postmodern age of relativism – was inaugurated by **Thomas Kuhn** (1922-95) in *The Structure of Scientific Revolutions* (1962). Kuhn was troubled by the "triumphalist" mode of teaching the history of science. Science was assumed to be always true and constantly progressing, a happy picture not challenged by the ordinary course of science.

But historians found that when a major advance is made, there is a more or less protracted period of debate before it is accepted. How can one explain this?

Worse, sometimes people who otherwise appear to be real scientists, deny what is later accepted as scientific truth. Could it be that even now, science is not protected from error, and some of its confident assertions could be false? The traditional historians' response to such a threat was generally to denigrate those scientists who were on the losing side as intellectually or morally defective.

The Paradigm Shift

Kuhn sensed that the traditional history of science was too simple. His study of Aristotle led him to the illuminating insight that each set of theories has its own validity. Out of this came his key idea of "paradigm" – the unquestionable basis on which "puzzle-solving normal science" is done, until there is a crisis resulting from the inability to progress and an accumulation of anomalies.

A "scientific revolution" then occurs, producing a new "incommensurable" paradigm. The switch from one to another is akin to a "conversion experience".

Give us a hand to shift this paradigm, will yer?

This very plausible account left the questions of truth and progress both wide open. By one reading of Kuhn, science was relative and indeed arbitrary.

The Popper school recognized the ideological implications of Kuhn's philosophy and attempted to combat it. But it was too late. Out of the turbulent 1960s came **Paul Feyerabend** (1924-94) who finished off the classical epistemological approach to the understanding of science.

He argued that science had replaced theology as the main enemy of liberty.

In his *Against Method* (1975), Feyerabend showed that any given principle of scientific method or scientific good practice had been broken by some great scientist – Galileo was a good anarchistic example. Indeed, there was no such thing as "scientific method".

After Feyerabend, the leading edge passed from philosophy to the behavioural studies of science. The demystifying, debunking tone became dominant. By the end of the 1970s, cultural studies of science had developed into a fully-fledged subject going under various rubrics: "science, technology and society", "science policy studies" and "social studies of science".

In the 1980s, Bruno Latour and Steve Woolgar inaugurated a new wave of cultural studies of science with the publication of *Laboratory Life* (1979), subtitled "Social Construction of Scientific Facts". This was an explicitly ironic study, with the investigators adopting a pseudo-naive pose.

As to "facts" or "progress", either as products of the activity or as motivations of the tribesmen-scientists, these entered the story only incidentally. Latour and Woolgar were followed by a host of other scholars – most notably Karin Knorr-Cetina and Steve Fuller – studying the anthropology, sociology, religiosity and culture of science.

Science Defended ...

Spring/Summer 1996. Copyright © 1996 by Duke
6/47, Vol. 14, No... Press.

There had to be a reaction from the defenders of science. Constructivists, deconstructionists, feminists, any sort of -ists who reflected critically on science, were lumped together as the enemy in the counter-attacks led by Paul Gross and Norman Leavitt in their *Higher Superstition: The Academic Left and Its Quarrels with Science* (1994). Such a shotgun approach could not have a sharp focus. But this was eventually supplied by a physicist. Alan D. Sokal published a famous hoax paper in the respectable journal *Social Text* (1996). Sokal pretended to write about quantum gravity but made absurd claims, gave wrong facts and misrepresented theories, appropriated arguments from a whole plethora of writers who have worked on the sociology and cultural studies of science, and wrapped his entire paper in the jargon of cultural studies.

Transgressing the Boundaries

TOWARD A TRANSFORMATIVE HERMENEUTIC OF QUANTUM GRAVITY

Alan D. Sokal

Transgressing disciplinary boundaries ... [is] a subversive undertaking since it is likely to violate the sanctuaries of accepted ways of perceiving. Among the most fortified boundaries have been those between the natural sciences and the humanities.
—Valerie Greenberg, *Transgressive Readings*

The struggle for the transformation of ideology into critical science ... proceeds on the foundation that the critique of all presuppositions of science and ideology must be the only absolute principle of science.
—Stanley Aronowitz, *Science as Power*

There are many natural scientists, and especially physicists, who continue to reject the notion that the disciplines concerned with social and cultural criticism can have anything to contribute, except perhaps peripherally, to their research. Still less are they receptive to the idea that the very foundations of their worldview must be revised or rebuilt in the light of such criticism. Rather, they cling to the dogma imposed by the long post-Enlightenment hegemony over the Western intellectual outlook, which can be summarized briefly as follows: that there exists an external world, whose properties are independent of any individual human being and indeed of humanity as a whole; that these properties are encoded in "eternal" physical laws; and that human beings can obtain reliable, albeit imperfect and tentative, knowledge of these laws by hewing to the "objective" procedures and epistemological strictures prescribed by the (so-called) scientific method.

But deep conceptual shifts within twentieth-century science have undermined this Cartesian-Newtonian metaphysics (Heisenberg 1958; Bohr 1963); revisionist studies in the history and philosophy of science have cast further doubt on its credibility (Kuhn 1970; Feyerabend 1975; Latour 1987; Aronowitz 1988b); and most recently feminist and poststructuralist critiques have demystified the substantive content of mainstream Western scientific practice, revealing the ideology of domination concealed behind the façade of "objectivity" (Merchant 1980; Keller 1985; Harding 1986, 1991). It has thus become increasingly apparent that physical "reality," no less than social "reality," is at bottom a social and linguistic construct; that scientific "knowledge," far from being objective ...

> **No one noticed my hoax until it was too late — thus proving that things in cultural studies of science had become so relative that anyone could say anything and get away with it!**

> Sokal even takes a pot-shot at me!

AUTHOR

... And Science (de)Constructed

Meanwhile, the main thesis of the cultural studies of science has been consolidated in the following formula: scientific knowledge is socially and culturally constructed, not discovered.

These assertions have radically transformed our understanding of science, making it impossible for science to recover its earlier role as the only way to Truth and Civilization – whatever the outcome of the "Science Wars".

Technoculture Theory

The idea that technology is autonomous is central to modernist thought. Technological determination presumes a linear, causal connection between advancements in technology and social progress. Technology itself is presumed neutral and free from all cultural and ideological contamination. This picture promotes a passive relationship between society and technology which prevents us from asking critical questions.

Technocultural theory asks these very questions. It has its roots in the "Science, Technology and Society Studies" (STSS) that first emerged in the 1960s and developed a variety of theoretical perspectives to demonstrate the social and cultural origins of technology. Specific technologies, STSS has shown, embody the social and cultural forces that lie behind their development.

These elements — which include lifestyles, ideas of nature and systems of thought — are encoded or represented in specific technological artefacts.

A computer, a supersonic jet or a CD player comes complete with an intrinsic cultural and social baggage.

The term "technoculture" itself emphasizes the deep connection between technology and culture and forces us to realize that the "technological" is seldom divorced from the "human".

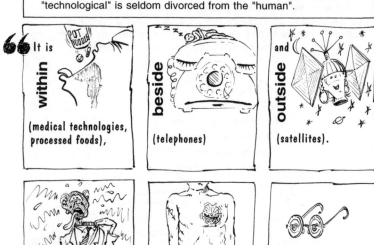

It is **within** (medical technologies, processed foods),

beside (telephones)

and **outside** (satellites).

Sometimes we inhabit it (a climate-controlled office space),

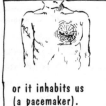 or it inhabits us (a pacemaker).

 Sometimes it seems to be an appendage or prosthetic (a pair of eye-glasses);

 at other times, human beings appear to serve as an appendage (as in an assembly line).

 Things and their events and states are complicated.

 Technologies often "relate" to us; and other times we relate to them.

Michael Menser and Stanley Aronowitz, in *Techno-Science and Cyber-Culture* (1996)

Technoculture theory – or the cultural studies of technology – investigates the complex relationship between technology and human beings to show how technological advances affect cultural spaces and who is socially, culturally and politically privileged with developments in technology. Technologies are often implicated in the production of myths in which patterns of domination and exploitation are regularly reproduced. Consider, for example, developments in computer technologies and the emergence of cyberspace. Glossy computer adverts project these developments as a gateway to unlimited vistas of connectivity and infotainment with an electronic democratic heaven just around the corner. Technoculture theory reveals the darker side of these developments.

A nightmare scenario of global consumerism ...

Increasing unemployment ...

Domination by surveillance and transnational corporations ...

Instead of ushering in an electronic democracy, cyberspace may catapult the world into a surreal mix of psychowar and corporate feudalism.

Haraway's Cyborgs

Donna Haraway is perhaps the best-known exponent of technoculture. In her celebrated book, *Simians, Cyborgs, and Women* (1991) – a powerful feminist critique of science and technology – she introduces the novel idea of cyborgs.

The boundaries between animal and human have been breached. In an era of many voices, the Other and the self are becoming one.

Organisms are no longer bodies of knowledge but biotic components, a kind of information-processing device. We are thus facing a new boundary between science fiction and social reality, the no-man's-land inhabited by cyborgs.

The term cyborg was coined in the 1960s by the American scientists Manfred Clynes and Nathan Kline to refer to the enhanced man who could survive the harsh extraterrestrial environment. Cyborgs were seen as cybernetic organisms, a result of a fusion between biology and technology. Haraway brings cyborgs to earth and defines them as "chimeras, theorized and fabricated hybrids of machine and organism", "a creature in a post-gender world" that is forged in particular historical and cultural practices.

These creatures are not reverent; they do not re-member the cosmos. They are wary of holism but needy for connection — they seem to have a natural feel for united front politics, but without the vanguard party.

We are all cyborgs now, Haraway contends, and might as well prepare ourselves for joint kinship with machines and not be afraid of partial identities and contradictory standpoints. Indeed, if we take responsibility for social relations of technology, we need no longer demonize it, but start "reconstructing the boundaries of daily life, in partial connection with others, in communication with all of our parts".

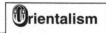

Orientalism

European imperialism of the 18th and 19th centuries ended chiefly in the second half of the 20th century when many former colonies obtained their independence. Imperialism had a profound effect on the subject people.

Juan Gimenez-Martin, *In the Harem*

A particular form in which imperialism survives today has come to be known as *Orientalism*, after the book published in 1978 by **Edward Said** (b. 1935), the Palestinian-American scholar, intellectual and activist. Orientalism has been described as the "grandest of all narratives" connecting Western knowledge and imperialism. Although Orientalism is regarded as a general theory of representation, it applies more specifically to Islam and the Muslims.

How did – and how does – Orientalism affect Western perceptions of Islam and the Middle East? Said points out that while the French and British were expanding their colonies, ideas about the colonized were also being formed. In a host of scholarly and literary works, the colonized were described as inferior, irrational, depraved, childlike. Said points out that:

The Oriental, as he or she came to be known, is represented and contained by these dominating frameworks.

Ideas about the Orient were formed in a context of domination and submission. Orientals could be understood, defined, controlled and manipulated by the dominant party.

This social, political, religious, academic and historical background to colonialism has a tremendous, persistent influence. It is in turn reinforced by and reinforces imperialism. Moreover, the values that enabled empire and imperial exploitations also shaped not only the fiction of early 20th century writers like Rudyard Kipling, E.M. Forster and Joseph Conrad, but even the works of those novelists we rarely associate with imperialism, such as Jane Austen, Charles Dickens, Thomas Hardy and Henry James.

More specifically, Said defines Orientalism in the following terms.

1. The classical tradition of studying a region by means of its languages and writings. Anyone who teaches, researches or writes about the Orient is an Orientalist. Said is concerned that Orientalism in this form lives on through its doctrines and theses, with the "expert Orientalist" as its main authority.

2. The second definition, related to this academic tradition, is "a style of thought based upon an ontological and epistemological distinction made between 'the Orient' and 'the Occident'". Said views these as fictions that gave rise to rhetoric of blame.

3. Orientalism, Said insists, always "overrode the Orient". As a system of thought, "it always rose from the specifically human detail to the general transhuman one; an observation about a tenth-century Arab poet multiplied itself into a policy towards (and about) the Oriental mentality in Egypt, Iraq or Arabia. Similarly, a verse from the Koran would be considered the best evidence of an ineradicable Muslim sensuality."

4. Finally, Said defines Orientalism as "the corporate institution for dealing with the Orient – dealing with it by making statements about it, authorizing views of it, describing it, by teaching it, settling it, ruling over it: in short, Orientalism as a Western style for dominating, restructuring and having authority over the Orient."

Forerunners to Orientalism

Edward Said was not the first to discuss Western images of the non-West or to introduce the notion of Orientalism. Over a decade before the publication of *Orientalism*, the Syrian scholar Abdul Lafit Tibawi had covered similar ground in his monograph, *English Speaking Orientalists* (1965). In *Europe and Islam* (1977), the Tunisian historian and philosopher Hichem Djait presented arguments and evidence about European representation of Islam remarkably similar to those of Said. And the Malaysian sociologist Syed Hussain Alatas in his seminal work, *The Myth of the Lazy Native* (1977)...

I outlined how the colonial powers constructed the image of the Malays, Filipinos and Javanese from the 16th to the 20th centuries and how these representations shaped the ideology of colonial capitalism.

Many other writers – amongst them Anwar Abel Malek, Abdullah Laroui, Talal Asad, K.M. Panikkar and Ramila Thapar – had also produced formidable texts on Orientalism before Said's *Orientalism*.

So, why did Edward Said become a *cause célèbre* while Tibawi, Hichem, Alatas and others remain largely ignored? For one thing, the location of these writers was important. Tibawi was working in the relatively obscure field of Islamic studies. Djait wrote in Arabic and lived in Tunis, although his work was translated first into French and later into English. Alatas was located in Singapore and doing unfashionable sociology from a Third World perspective.

Criticisms of Said

Said was located in New York and wrapped his theory in what was fast becoming the highly-fashionable field of textual theory. Although he was working in an already existing tradition, he brought a reading of **Michel Foucault** (1926-84) – the post-structuralist historian of ideas – to give old material a new universal twist: Orientalism was argued as a general theory of all representations of all non-Western cultures. Hence the difference: location, fashion, generalization.

Responses to Said's approach include accusations that he has made a special case for the Middle East.

Other regions – Africa and Asia, for example – have suffered just as much.

He also blames the West for all Arab ills.

He examines the issues in purely literary terms that are too limiting and do not actually address real issues.

There is also a critique that turns his argument against him: if the Orient has been the object of the West and unable to represent itself, who is he to do the representing?

The most trenchant criticism of Said came from the British anthropologist **Ernest Gellner** (1926-95), with whom Said had a long-running battle, and the Indian Marxist scholar **Aijaz Ahmad**. Gellner argued that just because something is a product of imperialism, it does not mean that it is wrong or unjust, any more than something being non-colonial makes it right...

In his much-discussed book, *In Theory* (1992), Aijaz Ahmad accuses Said of having double standards on the European humanist tradition.

Said rejects humanism-as-history because Orientalism is a by-product of this tradition, but then appeals to the same tradition in his plea for resisting stereotypical representations of the non-West.

Said has similar double and contradictory standards on Foucault and certain right-wing writers on whom he relies for his analysis. Said, Ahmad writes, can "be contrary in the same text"! Finally, Ahmad accuses Said of not being very original and relying heavily on a host of writers without acknowledging his debt or the influence of these authors on his work.

ost-Colonial Discourse

Orientalism spawned a whole genre of critical writings known variously as post-colonial studies, post-colonial theory and post-colonial discourse. The term "post-colonial" does not imply "after colonialism".

The Indian feminist and member of the Subaltern Studies collective **Gayatri Spivak** is considered to be one of the most subversive post-colonial critics. An aggressive anti-historicist and translator of Jacques Derrida, Spivak argues against "hegemonic historiography" which, to take one example, presents Indian history as continuous and homogeneous in terms of heads of state and British administrators. Her aim is not so much to deconstruct imperial history but to destroy critical historical reasoning itself.

Spivak wants to relocate non-Western discourses in totally new spaces where heterogeneity is the norm and a new "worlding of the world" is created.

116

Moreover, for Spivak, radical criticism often reproduces imperialist assumptions. When Western feminists insist on promoting individualism and project feminism as necessary and good, they are unconsciously duplicating imperialist values.

Spivak also argues against making a virtue of continuous *difference*. Those who romanticize difference are guilty of reverse ethnocentrism.

The idolization of the natives is also a Western fantasy that sees them as a reservoir of goodness and an endless source of information.

This process also denies the non-Western cultures a chance to create their own worlds.

Homi Bhabha

The black British academic **Homi Bhabha** uses psychoanalysis to read the historical phenomenon of colonialism. The discourse of colonialism, argues Bhabha, has an inner psychological tension that ensures that the relationship between the colonial and the colonizing subjects is always ambivalent.

The depersonalized, dislocated colonial subject thus becomes an "incalculable object" that is always difficult to place.

Thus the very nature of the colonial power undermines its own authority and paradoxically can provide the means for native resistance.

Even the indoctrinated natives left behind by the colonial powers to continue their work in the former colonies reveal the ambivalence of the colonial discourse. In India, for example, the British left a whole class of brown Englishmen.

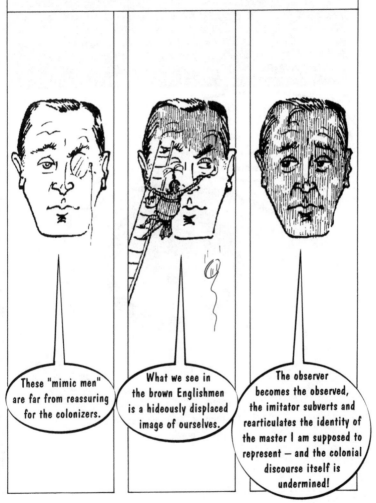

These "mimic men" are far from reassuring for the colonizers.

What we see in the brown Englishmen is a hideously displaced image of ourselves.

The observer becomes the observed, the imitator subverts and rearticulates the identity of the master I am supposed to represent — and the colonial discourse itself is undermined!

Liberal democracy or Marxist historicism, Bhabha further asserts, cannot cope with the diversity of cultures. Their tendency to universalize and historicize makes cultural diversity transparent and elusive. In any case, different cultures are "incommensurables" and cannot be categorized into universalist frameworks. Against this containment of cultures, Bhabha seeks, as the title of his book suggests, *The Location of Culture* (1994), a "third space". This new space is "hybridity". Hybridity not only displaces the history that creates it, but sets up new structures of authority and generates new political initiatives.

The process of cultural hybridity gives rise to something different, something new and unrecognizable, a new area of negotiation of meaning and representation.

Hybridity is thus a site of resistance, a "strategic reversal of the process of domination" that turns "the gaze of discriminated back upon the eye of the power".

Sara Suleri

The Pakistani-Welsh post-colonial critic **Sara Suleri** challenges the conventions of colonial discourse which separate the works of Western and non-Western writers. In her powerfully argued study, *The Rhetoric of English India* (1992), she asserts that both colonial writers and colonized writers collude in producing master narratives. Writers such as **Salman Rushdie** (b. 1947) and **V.S. Naipaul** (b. 1932) are seduced into a curious belief.

That literature can somehow rescue them from colonial consciousness.

Rushdie

Naipaul

She presents the idea of "English India" to emphasize that there is no distinction between colonial and post-colonial history and to show continuity between the Raj and modern India.

Race and Identity

The notions of race, identity and difference are central to cultural studies. It is now generally accepted that "race" is a socially constructed concept.

Racism developed as a set of ideologies and pseudo-scientific doctrines after the Renaissance, especially with the industrialization of Europe and the process of colonization. Racism became universal. Non-European peoples were despised as inferior and seen as material ripe for exploitation.

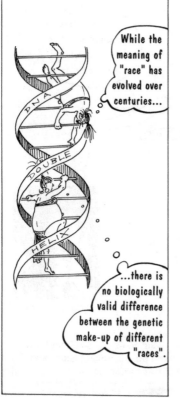

While the meaning of "race" has evolved over centuries...

...there is no biologically valid difference between the genetic make-up of different "races".

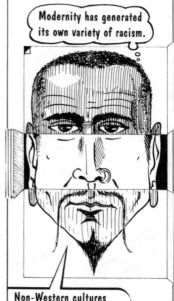

Modernity has generated its own variety of racism.

Non-Western cultures are often seen as obstacles to development, and this leads to racism against those seen as "outside modernity" or anti-modern.

Multiculturalism and its Critics

Multiculturalism is the common notion that describes diverse races living in pluralistic harmony. It sees diversity as plurality of identities and as "a condition of human existence". Within this pluralist framework, identity is regarded as the product of an assemblage of customs, practices and meanings, an enduring heritage and a set of shared traits and experiences.

As an approach to understanding diversity, multiculturalism has come under severe criticism.

Multiculturalism has tended to reproduce the "saris, samosas and steel bands syndrome" – that is, it focuses on superficial manifestations of culture and makes them exotic. It views different cultures in terms of how "different" they are from English culture, not on their own terms.

The critics of multiculturalism argue that identities are constituted by power relations. They are often defined in relation to outsiders – the Others. Western representations of race have created ethnic identities through novels, theatre, painting, films, television documentaries, music and photography.

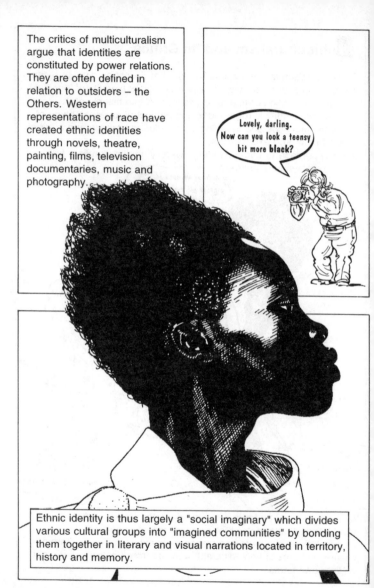

Lovely, darling. Now can you look a teensy bit more **black**?

Ethnic identity is thus largely a "social imaginary" which divides various cultural groups into "imagined communities" by bonding them together in literary and visual narrations located in territory, history and memory.

The British Asian sociologist **Ali Rattansi** argues that in racist cultures *ethnic* identities are *racialized*. This happens when popular or specialized biological discourses are combined with cultural markers such as a religion to "legitimate projects of subject formation, inclusion and exclusion, discrimination, inferiorization, exploitation, verbal abuse and physical harassment and violence". He points out that ethnic and racialized identities are always multiple and contradictory and marked by ambivalences.

Rasheed Araeen (b. 1935), British Asian artist.

I can say I'm Asian, Indian, Pakistani, British, European, Muslim, Oriental, secular, modernist, postmodernist ... But what do all these things mean? Do they define my identity? Can I accept all of them as part of my life, or must I choose one thing or another according to someone else's notion about my identity? I have no problem in saying that I'm all of these things, and perhaps none of these things at the same time.

ℭornel West

According to **Cornel West** (b. 1953), the Afro-American intellectual, identity is connected with affiliation – a longing to belong, to have security and safety. But it is also to do with death. People are willing to die for it, and sometimes identities are constructed with this in mind.

> We have, with our inevitable extinction, come up with a way of endowing ourselves with significance.

TOKEN BLACK

TOKEN OLD PERSON

TOKEN PUNK

TOKEN WOMAN

Identity is about binding people together, but also about being bound, often by "parochialist, narrow, xenophobic" notions.

But identity is also about resources and the systems generated to distribute them (or not, as the case may be). West gives the example of working-class people hit hard by taxes, exploited as a group, who scapegoat black people and women. Much "identity talk", West asserts, is usually about victims.

> Having a conference on race? Bring on the black folk. We do not want to invite some white racists so they can lay bare the internal dynamics of what it is to be a white racist.

TOKEN CHILD

TOKEN WORKING CLASS

TOKEN ASIAN

TOKEN REACTIONARY BIGOT

He insists that identity must be discussed from all angles, and that the role of whiteness, maleness and straightness must be examined in relation to blackness or gayness.

bell hooks

The Afro-American writer **bell hooks** – that's right, no capitals – emphasizes the direct link between identity and political struggle. She criticizes those who see cultural identity as "uncool" and a sign of political retreat.

The struggle for black identity is a practical intervention in political practice and an attempt to enable change.

She sees identity not as a constraint, but as a "stage in a process wherein one constructs radical black subjectivity", thus generating other options besides assimilation, imitation or rebellion.

The sense of deep alienation and powerlessness felt by black people in America leads to a yearning for change – change that can renew the black liberation struggle.

But renewal involves broadening the notions of black identity which, at present, are very narrow. They must be seen in their true complexity and variety. Black cultural criticism, hooks believes, can make a difference. But she laments the almost total absence of black female critics, despite a plethora of black women writing popular and literary fiction.

The greatest need of black people today is cultural criticism that can illuminate and enrich our understanding of the social formation of black identity, and the commodification of "blackness".

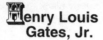enry Louis Gates, Jr.

What is black literature? What is black criticism? **Henry Louis Gates, Jr**. (b. 1950) is concerned with these questions. Are black critics in danger when they use literary theory that originates in Western European languages and literatures? Is this a form of intellectual servitude? Does the use of such theories, Gates asks, mar, violate or corrupt the original black text? Or is the black text in any way "pure" at all?

> Some black critics argue that black music and dance is "purer" than black literature which is an imitation of European and American literary conventions.

> "Blackness" does not exist as some mythical and mystical absolute, an entity so subtle and sublime that only black people could understand and decode its texts.

These "ideological shadows" have stunted black literature for two hundred years.

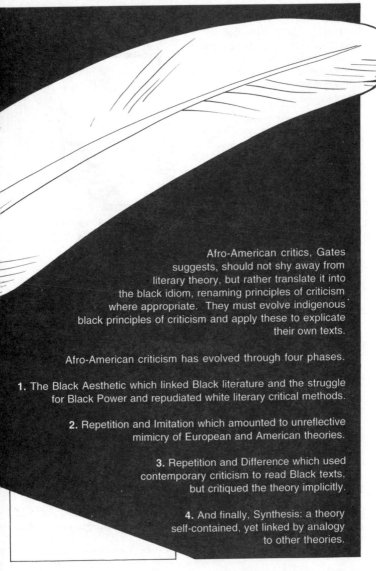

Afro-American critics, Gates suggests, should not shy away from literary theory, but rather translate it into the black idiom, renaming principles of criticism where appropriate. They must evolve indigenous black principles of criticism and apply these to explicate their own texts.

Afro-American criticism has evolved through four phases.

1. The Black Aesthetic which linked Black literature and the struggle for Black Power and repudiated white literary critical methods.

2. Repetition and Imitation which amounted to unreflective mimicry of European and American theories.

3. Repetition and Difference which used contemporary criticism to read Black texts, but critiqued the theory implicitly.

4. And finally, Synthesis: a theory self-contained, yet linked by analogy to other theories.

Gates's own literary history is taken from black rhetorical strategy called *signifyin*(g) and drawn entirely from the "Signifyin Monkey" tales. The figure of the Signifyin Monkey is...

"...the profane counterpart of Esu-Elegbara, the Yoruba sacred trickster who is truly pan-African, manifesting himself among the Cubans, the Haitians, the Brazilians. Hermes is his closest Western counterpart."

As I, Hermes, am to **hermeneutics**, so is Esu to the black art of interpretation, **Esu-"tufunaalo"**.

Signifyin(g) is a uniquely black rhetorical concept whereby a second statement or figure repeats, or tropes, or reverses the first. Its use as a figure for intertextuality allows critics to understand literary revision without resource to European themes and concepts.

Diaspora

Diaspora, from the Greek, means "dispersion". In its essential form, diaspora is a minority community living in exile. It involves the idea of home, from which the displacement occurs, and histories of gruelling journeys undertaken in the face of economic or political hardship. The most famous diaspora is, of course, that of the Jews.

We have forever been living in exile since our 6th century B.C. Babylonian captivity.

The Palestinian diaspora in the US is the most noted in recent history.

But nowadays there are diasporas everywhere. For instance, we Afro-Caribbeans in Britain.

South Asians in America.

Vast numbers of refugees from Africa living wherever we can find shelter.

Each community has its own historical experience and its own problems.

133

Diaspora Space

The diaspora exists with a number of tensions. There is the ever-present desire for "home" while making a new home. There are majority and minority tensions of power, of old (local) and new (often global) identities. Diaspora intellectuals are not only "natives" in a foreign land but also spokespersons for the natives back home. These tensions produce "diaspora space" where boundaries of inclusion and exclusion, of belonging and otherness, of "us" and "them", are contested.

But as a conceptual category, diaspora space is "inhabited" not just by the migrants but also those who have stayed behind and are constructed and represented as "indigenous".

The diaspora space is the site where the native is as much a diasporian as the diasporian is the native.

Avtar Brah
(British Asian Sociologist)

The black diaspora, as the black British sociologist Paul Gilroy argues, has succumbed to the absolutist notions of nationalism and cultural difference. In academia, black canons are constructed on exclusively national bases: African-American, Anglophone, and Caribbean.

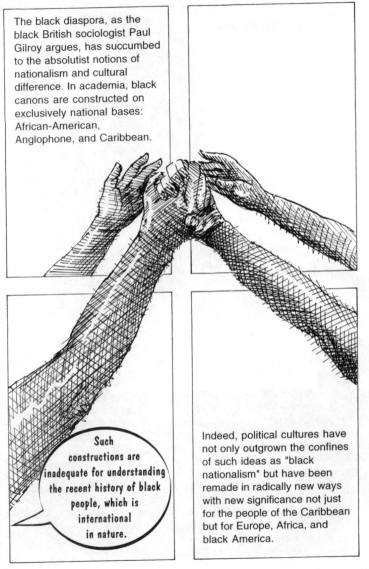

Such constructions are inadequate for understanding the recent history of black people, which is international in nature.

Indeed, political cultures have not only outgrown the confines of such ideas as "black nationalism" but have been remade in radically new ways with new significance not just for the people of the Caribbean but for Europe, Africa, and black America.

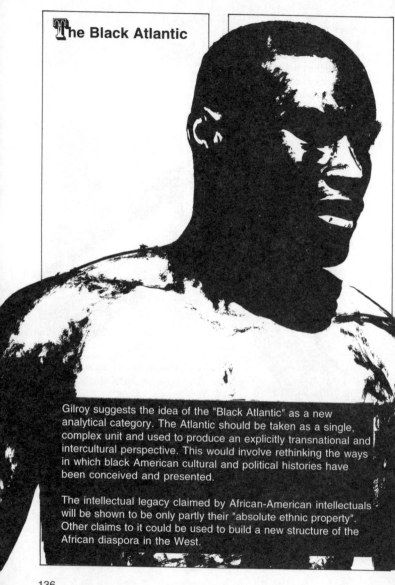

The Black Atlantic

Gilroy suggests the idea of the "Black Atlantic" as a new analytical category. The Atlantic should be taken as a single, complex unit and used to produce an explicitly transnational and intercultural perspective. This would involve rethinking the ways in which black American cultural and political histories have been conceived and presented.

The intellectual legacy claimed by African-American intellectuals will be shown to be only partly their "absolute ethnic property". Other claims to it could be used to build a new structure of the African diaspora in the West.

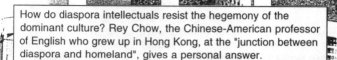

How do diaspora intellectuals resist the hegemony of the dominant culture? Rey Chow, the Chinese-American professor of English who grew up in Hong Kong, at the "junction between diaspora and homeland", gives a personal answer.

"The history of Hong Kong predisposes one to a kind of 'border' or 'parasite' practice — an identification with 'Chinese culture' but a distantiation from the Chinese Communist regime; a resistance against colonialism but an unwillingness to see the community's prosperity disrupted. The advantage of a continuous and complete institutional education, even when that education was British colonial and American, means that ... I have been 'subordinated'. Even though my 'personal' history is written with many forms of otherness, such otherness, when combined with the background of my education, is not that of the victim but of a specific kind of social power, which enables me to speak and write by wielding the tools of my enemies."

Rey Chow, *Writing Diaspora*, Indiana University Press, 1993.

Women and Gender

"Gender" has two meanings. The first is a contrast word to "sex" which depicts social construction as opposed to biological determination. The other meaning is any social construction involving the male/female distinction. This second definition came into use when feminists realized that society not only influences personality and behaviour, but also the ways in which the body appears.

If the body is seen through social interpretation, then sex is not something separate from gender but is only an artifice under it.

Culture is a place where the social arrangements of gender can be contested. Cultural ideologies and institutions reinforce the dualistic separation of male and female. This is particularly so for women's place in cultural *production* (as artists, authors, patrons, and members of cultural institutions) and in the dominant modes of cultural *representation*, such as literature and the visual arts, where the constructed notions of gender have a strong presence.

139

Women Take Issue

During the 1960s and 70s, when feminism was making its presence felt, most feminists viewed sex as a base upon which gender was constructed. Sex and Gender were different. One advantage of this position was that it enabled women to stress commonalties among women. It also enabled them to postulate differences.

> The body was viewed as a common rack upon which different societies could inflict different norms of behaviour or personality.

In the late 1970s, feminism confronted cultural studies directly. Or to use Stuart Hall's words...

> ...as a thief in the night, it broke in; interrupted, made an unseemly noise, seized the time, crapped on the table of cultural studies.

In *Women Take Issue* (1978), Women's Study Group attacked the male, middle-class bias of cultural studies.

In the early 1980s, feminism was itself challenged for its "heterosexism" by lesbians.

In the late 1980s and early 90s, it came under further attacks from black and non-Western women who challenged its Eurocentric perspectives.

One interpretation of these events is that feminism fragmented.

Alternatively, we can argue that there are different forms of *feminisms*.

From the perspective of cultural studies, feminist cultural politics can be broadly divided into (at least) five contesting categories.

1. Feminist liberal politics stresses the importance of equality and opportunity in such areas as employment, access to education and childcare.

> We emphasize the **individuality** of women without focusing on their differences from men.

2. Woman-centred cultural politics, on the other hand, concentrates on a perspective that privileges female difference.

> Our variety of cultural politics aims to rewrite women's history from **their** perspective.

3. Marxist feminists view gender as a cultural phenomenon. Differences in women's cultural practice are not seen as signs of essential differences between the sexes.

> Gender differences are explained in terms of how useful these differences are to **capitalism**.

In these first three categories, the biological male/female difference is maintained. But in the following two, male/female biological distinction is deliberately blurred.

143

4. In postmodern feminism, gender and race do not have a fixed meaning. Each individual is seen as a composite of elements from a range of available modes of subjectivity. While these elements may be contradictory in themselves, they are appropriate in different contexts. No one is naturally male or female. Femininity and masculinity are socially constructed and are a site of political struggle about meaning.

Postmodern feminists are not interested in creating or rediscovering "authentic" female expression, but in showing that social construction of gender involves power relations.

This approach is attacked by liberal, women-centred and Marxist feminists for destroying the very basis of the feminist movement and weakening women's unity. The postmodernists respond that their approach allows space for a variety of voices and new interpretations of identity.

5. Black and non-Western feminists concentrate on racism and colonialism, and view these as tools for understanding gender relations. For black women, race remains an essential form of oppression.

Non-Western feminism is thus grounded in histories of racism and imperialism, the recognition of the role of the modern state in perpetuating these and the identification of the difference, conflicts, and contradictions internal to non-Western societies and communities. Not surprisingly, the use of Western feminism as a yardstick, and the representation of non-Western feminists as merely victims, are strongly attacked by "Third World" feminists.

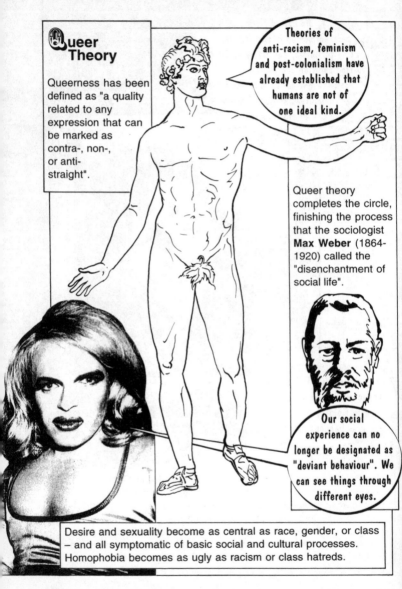

Queer Theory

Queerness has been defined as "a quality related to any expression that can be marked as contra-, non-, or anti-straight".

Theories of anti-racism, feminism and post-colonialism have already established that humans are not of one ideal kind.

Queer theory completes the circle, finishing the process that the sociologist **Max Weber** (1864-1920) called the "disenchantment of social life".

Our social experience can no longer be designated as "deviant behaviour". We can see things through different eyes.

Desire and sexuality become as central as race, gender, or class – and all symptomatic of basic social and cultural processes. Homophobia becomes as ugly as racism or class hatreds.

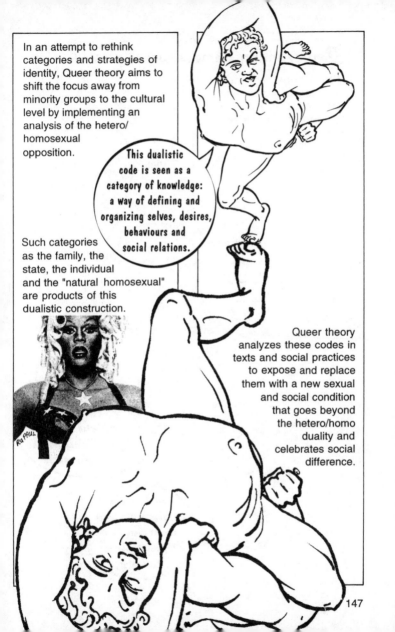

In an attempt to rethink categories and strategies of identity, Queer theory aims to shift the focus away from minority groups to the cultural level by implementing an analysis of the hetero/homosexual opposition.

This dualistic code is seen as a category of knowledge: a way of defining and organizing selves, desires, behaviours and social relations.

Such categories as the family, the state, the individual and the "natural homosexual" are products of this dualistic construction.

RU PAUL

Queer theory analyzes these codes in texts and social practices to expose and replace them with a new sexual and social condition that goes beyond the hetero/homo duality and celebrates social difference.

147

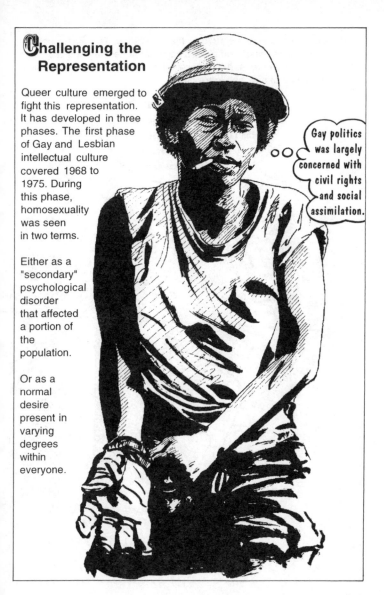

Challenging the Representation

Queer culture emerged to fight this representation. It has developed in three phases. The first phase of Gay and Lesbian intellectual culture covered 1968 to 1975. During this phase, homosexuality was seen in two terms.

Either as a "secondary" psychological disorder that affected a portion of the population.

Or as a normal desire present in varying degrees within everyone.

Gay politics was largely concerned with civil rights and social assimilation.

The second phase covers 1975 to the mid-1980s. This was a period of "community building" and politicization of the Lesbian and Gay movements. An increased tolerance within American society allowed the emergence of new gay intellectuals.

As academics and intellectuals, we rejected the theory of homosexual identity as a fixed, universally identical phenomenon.

The third stage began in the mid-1980s when the AIDS epidemic and the anti-gay backlash led by the New Right shattered illusions of an age of tolerance and understanding. This in turn prompted a renewal of radical confrontational politics.

The anti-gay backlash was seen as evidence of the success with which gay culture had managed to locate itself in the mainstream.

This success was evident in the marketing of gay-identified fashion.

The number of column inches devoted to gay interests in newspapers and magazines.

And the gay output of academic publishers.

A need was felt for a critical theory that linked gay affirmation with broad institutional change. The result was Queer theory, which settled into universities as the main sites of gay and lesbian discourses.

Queer theory has been criticized for "veiling" its own ethical base. Queer theorists, so the critics argue, have not provided an alternative social and moral articulation of difference. Moreover, the "historical" in Queer theory is reduced to the modern West or the period 1880-1980 in modern Western societies.

This means that non-Western cultures are almost totally ignored in Queer theory.

Indeed, many Queer theorists seem to be unaware that anything exists outside California!

153

Media and Culture

We live today in a multi-media world. "Multi" not just in the variety of messages, signifying systems and types of discourses hurled at us at great speed, but also in the actual forms of the media. We seek our information and entertainment – or "infotainment" – from...

BOOKS

RADIO

TELEVISION — TERRESTRIAL, SATELLITE, CABLE

PRESS

SHOCK HORROR PROBE

CINEMA

VIDEO

CASSETTES

LASERDISC

CDs

CD-ROMs

SOFTWARE

INTERNET

It's a world of complex interconnections and fragmentary discontinuities.

(CONSUMER)

There are four basic components to the media industry that packages the messages and the products.

✂ The message or the product itself.

☎ The audiences who imbibe the message and consume the products.

❀ The ever-changing technology that shapes both the industry and the way the message is communicated.

✥ And the final look of the product.

These components, interacting simultaneously in a surrounding social and cultural world, occupy a space that is constantly being contested.

The changing contours of this space can lead to different patterns of domination and representation.

Film and television have their own language with distinct syntax and grammar.

This grammar consists of such familiar elements as cuts, close-ups, the two shot, the long shot, zoom-in, zoom-out, fade, dissolve, slow motion, speeded-up action, special effects.

TITLE CULTURAL STUDIES FOR BEGINNERS

DIRECTOR APPIGNANESI

WRITER ZIA

DESIGNER LOON

TAKE 156

But that language also includes more subtle codes of representation which range in complexity from literal visual depiction to the most abstract and arbitrary symbols and metaphors.

The simplest level of representation involves little more than the portrayal of "real world" information – a man walking in the street. But the language of film comes into play as soon as you want to do more: show a close-up of his face, a front shot walking towards the camera, a back shot walking away from the camera, a long shot to show where he is actually walking, and so on. The composite representation will edit all these different shots into one sequence. The *sequence* is thus the basic element of the moving picture.

Media representation can also involve linguistic and visual symbolic forms that encode the message being conveyed.

At its most elementary level, a "voice-over" may simply describe the on-screen objects and action — the form common in most documentaries.

But voice-over and dialogue can also encode literary meanings, as when a fade is accompanied by the line: "once upon a time".

Visual metaphors often allude to real world objects and symbols and connote social and cultural meanings.

The most famous representation of sex is a train entering a tunnel; the most common, waves splashing on the rocks.

*There's always one, isn't there?

Media Codes

Media codes can be internalized as forms of *mental* representations. Thus people can, and often do, think in moving pictures with flashbacks, fast and slow motion, and dissolving into another time, another place. But these codes can also be a subtle form of advertising.

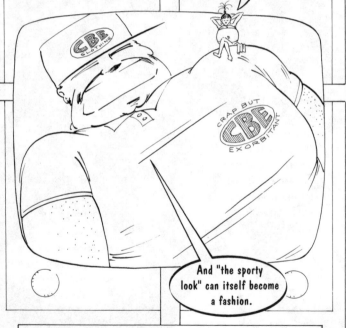

Codes feed on codes and the world becomes awash with coded individuals.

But however natural it all looks, it is socially and culturally constructed. Television news, for example, despite its immediacy, is a mammoth feat of social construction.

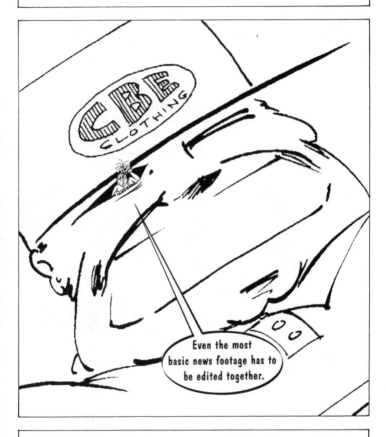

And even that "live link", the on-the-spot report from "Our Correspondent", may have been manufactured at the head office and fed back to the correspondent who is simply reading from an autocue. All news is professional construction of social reality.

The Basic Issues of Representation

From the perspective of race and culture, we need to ask how good and convincing an account of cultural reality is. There are three basic issues.

First, there is the question of inclusion.

Do media reports and products include images, views, backgrounds and cultures of different racial groups?

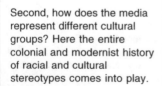

Second, how does the media represent different cultural groups? Here the entire colonial and modernist history of racial and cultural stereotypes comes into play.

Third, what role do people from different cultural groups play in shaping the end products – what control do they have in the process of production?

Globalization

In a global multi-media world, it is even more important that all cultures have rights to faithful and respectful representation. But reliable representation and adequate access cannot be gained without struggle.

The market mechanism often favours the profitable recycling of old stereotypes and clichés and threatens pluralistic representation.

REGIONAL CONFERENCE on Globalisation

1-6 JULY 1997 • SHAH ALAM • MALAYSIA

the perceptions, experiences and responses of the religious traditions and cultural communities in the Asian Pacific region

And the ever-increasing tendency on the part of the global networks to speak on behalf of their home base – particularly the USA and Britain – involves the perpetuation of the dominance of the West and subordination of the small, poorer nations. The process that is transforming the world into the proverbial "global village", rapidly shrinking distances, compressing space and time, is known as **globalization**.

Globalization is being ushered in by three significant general trends.

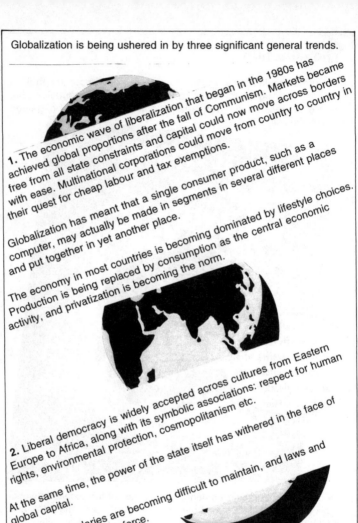

1. The economic wave of liberalization that began in the 1980s has achieved global proportions after the fall of Communism. Markets became free from all state constraints and capital could now move across borders with ease. Multinational corporations could move from country to country in their quest for cheap labour and tax exemptions.

Globalization has meant that a single consumer product, such as a computer, may actually be made in segments in several different places and put together in yet another place.

The economy in most countries is becoming dominated by lifestyle choices. Production is being replaced by consumption as the central economic activity, and privatization is becoming the norm.

2. Liberal democracy is widely accepted across cultures from Eastern Europe to Africa, along with its symbolic associations: respect for human rights, environmental protection, cosmopolitanism etc.

At the same time, the power of the state itself has withered in the face of global capital.

Territorial boundaries are becoming difficult to maintain, and laws and regulations difficult to enforce.

Consequences of Globalization

Globalization tends to maintain the well-known patterns of Western economic and cultural imperialism. It promotes a dominant set of cultural practices and values – one vision of how life is to be lived at the expense of all others. And it has serious practical consequences.

It erodes non-Western local traditions and cultural practices.

It often kills local film and television industries which are so vital for promoting indigenous cultures.

It has led to the displacement of large numbers of people from their homes in Asia, Africa and Latin America to the West as either refugees or labour migrants.

But globalization is not a one-way process. It is not a process that is firmly in the economic and cultural grip of the West. The emergence of the highly competitive and advanced economies of South East Asia owes a great deal to globalization. Non-Western cultures are also having a reverse impact (although not on the same scale) on the West.

The emergence of Indian music on the global scale, for example, is changing musical tastes in the West.

Resisting Globalization

Globalization is also being resisted. For example, a network of intellectuals in Asia has not only organized grass-roots movements against various aspects of globalization but has also launched onslaughts on its theoretical elements. The "Asian values" debate in South East Asia has led to the questioning of liberal democracy as a universal form of governance. The Malaysian intellectual Chandra Muzaffar has attacked the very notion of human rights as the most evolved form of Western imperialism.

The Western liberal humanist notion of human rights is in fact (as I say in my book), **Human Wrongs** (1996).

Like Muzaffar, many non-Western intellectuals favour a discourse of human dignity based on the right to food, housing, basic sanitation and the preservation of one's own identity and culture.

Globalization may itself be undermined by the emergence of the Asian civilizations. This is the argument of *The Asian Renaissance* (1996) by the Malaysian politician and intellectual, Anwar Ibrahim.

This renaissance could lead to a symbiosis between East and West, replacing globalization with a **"global convivencia"**.

That is, a more harmonious and enriching experience of living together among people of diverse religions and cultures.

Global futures are thus more radically open than the process of globalization suggests.

Where is Cultural Studies Going?

Cultural studies started as a dissenting intellectual tradition outside academia, dedicated to exposing power in all its cultural forms. But it has now become a discipline and a part of the academic establishment and its power structure.

Only in the Indian Subcontinent, cultural studies still functions as an independent, but highly diverse, intellectual movement.

By being successfully domesticated in the knowledge industry, cultural studies has become too abstract and too technical, divorced from the lives and realities of the people it is supposed to be empowering, and on whose behalf it was to develop strategies for resistance and survival.

Its amorphous character means that almost anything can be, and often is, justified as "cultural studies". There seems to be little or no quality control. Moreover, certain segments of cultural studies appear to strive towards banality. It is one thing to study popular culture. It is quite another to romanticize junk and give it academic respectability. Meaningless "textual criticism" of music videos, pop culture and youth style is undermining the importance of cultural studies and the groundbreaking work already achieved in the field.

The legitimacy that cultural studies provides for infantile Western culture has a detrimental effect on Third World societies.

Respectable social scientists in places as distant as Delhi and Taiwan spend their time studying, teaching and defending Western junk at the expense of their own rich cultural heritage.

Exported Anglocentric cultural studies thus retraces the routes of British colonialism and reconstructs the Empire.

Champions of cultural studies should not make claims on its behalf that cannot be substantiated.

It does not give meaning and direction to those who follow or use it.

Cultural studies is not an ideology. It is not a religion.

It does not, and cannot, teach us how to live a good, moral life.

What it can do is help us to understand the mechanisms of cultural power and find ways and means to resist them. That's all.

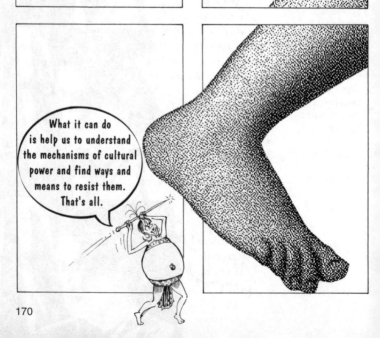

As a discipline, cultural studies is in danger of losing its E.DGE

It could simply dissolve into another discipline like sociology, anthropology or psychology. That would be a great shame. However, as a collective term for a number of diverse and often contentious intellectual endeavours that expose power in all its ubiquitous forms, cultural studies has a great future.

As a dissenting movement, cultural studies can remain open to unexpected, unimagined, uninvited possibilities – especially those that come from outside the West.

And, only as an intellectual movement of genuine dissent, in all its forms, can cultural studies fulfil its original promise.

DOWN WITH

Further Reading

The literature of cultural studies is notorious for being voluminous, impenetrable and trite. But there *are* important and good books out there. Here is a brief guide for the discerning.

Some of the general readers on cultural studies are surprisingly good, if a bit bulky. The best is **Cultural Studies** edited by Lawrence Grossberg, Cary Nelson and Paula Treicher (Routledge, London 1992).

There is no real substitute for reading the British "founding fathers": Richard Hoggart, **The Uses of Literacy** (Penguin, London 1958); Raymond Williams, **Culture and Society 1780-1950** (Penguin, London 1966, first published 1958); and the groundbreaking E.P. Thompson, **The Making of the English Working Class** (Penguin, London 1978, first published 1963). Students and friends of **Stuart Hall** (Routledge, London 1996) provide a highly abstract introduction to his thought and life in the guise of "critical dialogues in cultural studies".

Graeme Turner provides an excellent introduction to **British Cultural Studies** (Routledge, London 1990). Jill Forbes and Michael Kelly give an enthralling tour of **French Cultural Studies** (Oxford University Press, Oxford 1995). A worthy discussion of issues in Canadian cultural studies can be found in **Relocating Cultural Studies**, edited by Valda Blundell, John Shepherd and Ian Taylor (Routledge, London 1993). **What is Cultural Studies?**, edited by John Storey, (Edward Arnold, London 1996) contains some good papers on American and Australian cultural studies.

For those who want to know more about Louis Althusser, try **Reading Capital** (New Left Books, London 1970), or the more accessible **For Marx** (Penguin University Books, London 1969 or Vintage Books, New York 1970). James Joll gives a good short account of Antonio Gramsci in **Gramsci** (Fontana Modern Masters, London 1977); but you should try Gramsci himself, in **Selections from the Prison Notebooks** (Lawrence & Wishart, London 1971).

The dazzling brilliance of Ashis Nandy can be sampled in **The Intimate Enemy** (Oxford University Press, Delhi 1983); **A Secret History of Our Desires** (Zed, London 1997) entertainingly examines the influence of Indian cinema both in India and on the Asian community in Britain. Vinay Lal's **South Asian Cultural Studies** (Manohar, Delhi 1996) provides a bibliographical map of the thriving cultural studies industry in the Subcontinent.

An insightful discussion of post-colonialism can be found in Robert Young's **White Mythologies** (Routledge, London 1990). **The Post-Colonial Reader**, edited by Bill Ashcroft, Gareth Griffiths and Helen Tiffin (Routledge, London 1995) provides key writings of influential figures in one (very large) volume. If you haven't read Edward Said's **Orientalism** (Routledge, London 1978) where have you been? It should, however, be read in conjunction with Aijaz Ahmad's penetrating critique, **In Theory** (Verso, London 1992) and Sara Suleri's **The Rhetoric of English India** (University of Chicago Press, 1992).

Sandra Harding's anthology, **The Racial Economy of Science** (Indiana University Press, Bloomington 1993), is essential reading for understanding how science shapes attitudes, culture and economy. Michael Adas' **Machines as the Measure of Men** (Cornell University Press, London 1989) gives a penetrating insight into "science, technology and the ideologies of dominance". In **Science** (Open University, Milton Keynes 1997) Steve Fuller shows what science may look like to a Martian anthropologist.

A good overview of the cultural studies of technology is found in **Techno-Science and Cyber-Culture**, edited by Stanley Aronowitz, Barbara Matinson and Michael Menser (Routledge, London 1996). Ziauddin Sardar and Jerome Ravetz provide an accessible introduction to the cultural politics of **Cyberfutures** (Pluto Press, London 1996). But there are no substitutes for Donna Haraway, **Simians, Cyborgs and Women** (Free Association Books, London 1991).

Henry Louis Gates Jr.'s **Figures in Black** (Oxford University Press, Oxford 1987) takes issue with the notion of black literature as social realism. **Black Literature and Literary Theory**, edited by Gates (Routledge, London 1994) contains several noteworthy attempts to delineate the boundaries of black criticism. **Beyond Eurocentrism and Multiculturalism**, 2 volumes, (Common Courage Press, Monroe, Maine 1993) brings together the best of Cornel West. The best essays of bell hooks are collected in **Yearnings: Race, Gender, and Cultural Politics** (South End Press, Boston, Mass. 1990).

The Identity in Question, edited by John Rajchman (Routledge, London 1995) leads an informed expedition through the thorny issues of selfhood. **Racism, Modernity and Identity**, edited by Ali Rattansi and Sally Westwood (Polity Press, Oxford 1994) is an engaging anthology.

Eve Kosofsky Sedgwick's **Epistemology of the Closet** (Penguin, Harmondsworth 1990) is a landmark introduction to Queer theory. **Queer Theory/Sociology**, edited by Steven Seidman (Blackwell, Oxford 1996) contains some illuminating papers on the construction of homosexual identity.

Avtar Brah's **Cartographies of Diaspora** (Routledge, London 1996), Raymond Chow's **Writing Diaspora** (Indiana University Press, Bloomington 1993) and Paul Gilroy's **The Black Atlantic** (Verso, London 1993) provide excellent insights into Asian, Chinese and Black diasporas in the West.

Glenn Jordan and Chris Weedon's **Cultural Politics** (Blackwell, Oxford 1995) gives a comprehensive account of "class, gender, race and the postmodern world". **Feminine Sentences** by Janet Wolff (Polity Press, Oxford 1990) contains some penetrating words on women and culture.

Getting the Message: News, Truth and Power, edited by John Eldridge (Routledge, London 1993) summarizes decades of research by the Glasgow University Media Group. **The Media Reader**, edited by Manuel Alvarado and John Thompson (BFI, London 1990) provides a sensual tour of the pleasures and expectations of films and television.

Malcolm Waters makes **Globalisation** (Routledge, London 1995) relatively palatable. John Tomlinson gives a very clear account of **Cultural Imperialism** (Pinter, London 1991). And Ziauddin Sardar's **Postmodernism and the Other** (Pluto, London 1997) tackles "the new imperialism of Western culture". Anwar Ibrahim, **The Asian Renaissance** (Times Books, Kuala Lumpur 1996) provides a perspective from a different culture.

Index

Biographies

Ziauddin Sardar was not asked to play cricket for Pakistan. So, in an attempt to become an "organic intellectual", he became a writer, broadcaster and cultural critic. He has written *Introducing Muhammad*, *Chaos* and *Mathematics*, *Postmodernism and the Other* and numerous other books. Sometimes he visits Middlesex University as a professor of science and technology policy.

Borin Van Loon seems to move between the disparate spheres of art, philosophy, and economic determinism with alarming ease. Having recently directed his first full-length feature: "Eraserhead II — Revenge Of The Pencil", he has divided his time between L.A., Bangkok and Saxmundham, with some really exciting projects in development. Before embarking on his new production of "The Ring" cycle, he is currently in the fastness of his country estate finishing his novel.* He also has a rich and detailed fantasy life.

(*Which one is he reading? ⓒDorothy Parker)

Acknowledgements

We would like to thank our team of researchers:-
  Gail Boxwell and Merryl Wyn Davies - *For their invaluable interference in the writing of the text*
  Don Bloater - *Signifiers (Executive Head)*
  Clare de Loon - *Fragmentary discontinuities (Asia and Ipswich)*
  Max Miller - *Smartarse one-liners*
  Lauren Ban Foon - *Chimerical psychowar pictorialities*
  Jeroen Anthoniszoon Van Aken - *Epistemological holography (Belgium)*
  Don Van Vliet - *Diasporal colourist (Mojave Desert)*
  Aristotle Plato III - *Anagramatist / Scissors*
  Red Lal - *Subterranean activities*
  The Brothers Quaygrip - *Cell-tracers (Bermondsey and Toronto)*
  Percy Svankmajer - *Paradigm shifter (Tooting Bec)*
  Pomo I. Ronist - *Hegemonic historiography*
  e.e. lowercase - *gaffer tape*
  Stanley Stainless - *Pen Nibs*
  Takeo Hideo - *Yokuza bodyart (Kyoto)*